MITIGATION OF
CONSTRUCTION IMPACT
ON ARCHAEOLOGICAL REMAINS

Volume 1: Main report

Published by the Museum of London Archaeology Service for English Heritage
Copyright ' English Heritage 2004

ISBN 1-901992-41-1

Typesetting and design by Susan Banks (MoLAS)
Production by Tracy Wellman (MoLAS)
Copy editing by Monica Kendall

MITIGATION OF
CONSTRUCTION IMPACT
ON ARCHAEOLOGICAL REMAINS

Volume 1: Main report

M J Davis, K L A Gdaniec, M Brice and L White
(with contributions by C A I French and R Thorne)

UNIVERSITY OF
CAMBRIDGE

ENGLISH HERITAGE

Address for correspondence:

Mr M J Davis
239 High Street
Cottenham
Cambs. CB4 8QP
Email: mat.cath@dial.pipex.com

1	2

3	4

Cover illustrating redevelopment of the Anchor Terrace site, London, on which remains of the Globe Theatre are located.

Photos:
1 Eighteenth-century brick remains thought to be from a former brewery on the site
2 Reuse of foundations by the formation of minipiles through a redundant brick foundation base
3 Installation of an impermeable membrane as part of a covering mitigation strategy
4 Completion of the new development including flats and a commemorative area identifying the position of remains from the Globe Theatre

Photos courtesy of Hunting Technical Services

CONTENTS

FIGURES

TABLES

ACKNOWLEDGEMENTS

The study was commissioned by English Heritage, whose members contributed valuable information, help and guidance. We are particularly grateful to Sue Cole, Mike Corfield, Tim Williams, Terry Girdler and Steven Brocklehurst who acted as the monitoring committee for the study.

This report and the supplementary report has been prepared by Hunting Technical Services (HTS) and Cambridge Archaeological Unit (CAU). The project team consisted of Mat Davis (HTS), Kasia Gdaniec (CAU), Mike Brice (affiliate of HTS), Lee White (CAU), Wai-Ming Lee (HTS) and David Barr (HTS), with additional contributions from Charles French (University of Cambridge) and Robert Thorne (Alan Baxter & Associates).

The data collection would not have been possible were it not for the response of those who took the time to fill in the questionnaire. A list of all organisations and individuals originally contacted is in Volume 2 of this study (database manual). Those who responded were: (Development Control:) Birmingham City Council; Chester City Council Chester; Cornwall County Council; East Sussex County Council; Hertfordshire County Council; Humberside Archaeology Partnership; Isle of Wight County Council; North Kesteven District Council; North Yorkshire County Council; City of Plymouth Museums & Art Gallery; Southwark Council London; Staffordshire County Council; Suffolk County Council; Tees Archaeology; Winchester Museum Service; Wiltshire County Council Library & Museum Services; York City Council. Greater London Archaeological Advisory Service. (Contract Units and Consulting Bodies:) ARCUS Research; Archaeological Project Services; Avon Archaeological Unit; Cambridge Archaeological Unit; Cambridgeshire County Council Archaeological Field Unit; City of Lincoln Archaeology Unit; Cotswold Archaeological Trust; Earthworks Archaeological Services; Gifford and Partners Consulting; Huntings Technical Services Ltd; Lancaster University Archaeological Unit; Mills Whipp Partnership; Museum of London Archaeology Service; Northamptonshire Archaeological Unit; Sir William Halcrow & Partners; S E Archaeological Services; Surrey County Archaeology Unit; The Trust for Thanet Archaeology; Wardell Armstrong Consultants; Worcester County Archaeological Service; W S Atkins Consultants Ltd.

Due to time and/or cost constraints some responses were in the form of lists rather than questionnaires. Lists were submitted by: Essex Field Archaeology Group; Fenland Archaeological Trust; Hampshire County Council; Hereford & Worcester County Council; Northamptonshire Heritage; Museum of London Archaeology Service; York City Council.

We also thank those individuals who generously provided time to answer our questions personally in relation to the questionnaires and case studies, or who provided information for the bibliography. These include Mike Griffiths, Mike Griffiths & Associates; John Oxley, York City Council; Mike Morris, Chester City Council; David Evans, Humberside Archaeology Partnership; Paul Bennett, Canterbury Archaeological Trust; Hal Dalwood, Hereford & Worcester County Council; Ian Oxley, St Andrews University Archaeological Diving Unit; Peter Hinton, MoLAS; David Bone and Trevor Holmes, Posford Duvivier and Clay Mathers, Centre for Cultural Site Preservation Technology, Vicksburg, USA.

The Project Management team at MoLAS generously supplied details and useful discussion on a variety of strategies used in the City and Boroughs of London which, in effect, cover all aspects of construction mitigation and its route. We gratefully acknowledge their assistance in this project: Robin Densem, George Dennis, Paul Falcini, Al Green, Mike Hutchinson, Sophie Jackson, Gillian King, Dick Malt, Simon Mason, Geoffrey Potter, Angus Stephenson and Taryn Nixon. MoLAS also kindly supplied photographic evidence of construction processes and site vulnerability to illustrate appropriate points in the text.

The text was edited by Monica Kendall. Design and typesetting was by Susan Banks (MoLAS) and production by Tracy Wellman (MoLAS).

EXECUTIVE SUMMARY

Many engineering operations used during the course of a construction project have the potential to impact seriously on important archaeological remains. A real concern exists within the archaeological community and construction industry regarding the effectiveness of mitigation strategies frequently implemented to reduce or prevent such impacts, and thus enable the preservation *in situ* of archaeological remains. This concern is heightened by the fact that the effects of construction operations on different burial environments are at present poorly understood.

As a first step towards improving this situation, English Heritage commissioned this *Mitigation of construction impact on archaeological remains*. The study presents descriptions of operations typically employed during the course of a development, from the various groundworks required during the pre-construction stage, through to the potentially more damaging operations of construction stage, as well as

maintenance activities of the post-construction stage, which are seldom monitored. Mitigation options designed to reduce, avoid or limit damage or disturbance are also suggested, alongside strategies designed to enable preservation *in situ* of archaeological remains (avoidance, containment or reburial). The effects of various construction operations upon different burial-environment regimes are discussed, and avenues of further research suggested to enhance our understanding of the subject.

A second aspect to this study has been the compilation of a database of archaeological and construction sites where the preservation of archaeological remains has taken place. This database will be periodically updated by English Heritage, providing a valuable research tool for use when devising new mitigation strategies.

1.0 INTRODUCTION

1.1 Background and objectives

Archaeological considerations have been incorporated into construction and engineering programmes for at least two decades now, more significantly since the publication of Planning Policy Guidance Note 16 (*Archaeology and planning*, DoE 1990). This document places great emphasis on the physical preservation *in situ* of important archaeological remains by the use of positive management and sympathetic engineering designs, and yet the overall impacts of construction on archaeological remains are not fully understood. The urgency to address this gap in our knowledge is illustrated by the *Monuments at risk survey* which revealed that road building and construction (property development and urban expansion) accounted for 36 per cent of observed cases of wholesale archaeological monument destruction (Darvill and Fulton 1998). These figures do not take into account demolition and building alterations which can account for a further 20 per cent of all monuments destroyed. While experiments have been conducted to test the effects of, for example, compression or compaction of buried objects or soil layers from heavy machinery or earthen ramps, these have been mainly conducted in well-prepared arenas – 'open-air laboratories' – in which all manner of connected tests combine to produce unequivocal results of these effects (eg Bell et al 1996; US Army Engineer Waterways Experiment Station 1992). However, they do not adequately reflect conditions likely to be encountered on a British development site. In contrast to this, casual observations on redevelopment sites form the bulk of current knowledge regarding a wider range of construction effects than have been tested for. In other words, deep foundations laid during the last major campaign of development in the 1960s, a time which seldom saw archaeological involvement during the planning or, indeed, construction stages, are occasionally excavated in new redevelopments in which the direct and indirect effects of construction methods are being realised (eg pile grids causing archaeological damage and chance preservation at 1 Poultry, London; Schofield and Malt 1996).

To redress this situation, English Heritage commenced a period of crucial research and experimentation work into the effects and impacts of construction on archaeological remains,

and in programmes of monitored burial environments and hydrological regimes. Specific environment transformation problems are also being researched, and applications are being made to the science-based archaeological committee of the Natural Environment Research Council (NERC) for such a thematic research programme. This research will seek to examine all aspects of archaeological conservation and its implications for archaeological heritage management, and the results will hopefully be able to demonstrate the particular effects that construction processes are thought to have on archaeological and environmental remains.

This English Heritage-commissioned *Mitigation of construction impact on archaeological remains* extends the theme of a conference held in 1996 (Corfield et al 1998). The conference highlighted the current problems in British planning and development archaeology, relating to the justification of constraints imposed on some developments, and the assumed impact of certain construction activities on sites of archaeological importance. This study aims to improve an understanding of the variety of impacts on buried archaeological remains and so enable more informed and efficient management decisions to be made. In particular, the study aims to suggest mitigation strategies in order to avoid or minimise construction impacts which may compromise the objective of preservation *in situ*.

This study attempts to achieve the following objectives specified by English Heritage:

1 Broadly categorise types of below-ground archaeological sites, structures and deposits in England.

2 Produce an easy-to-understand guide to engineering and construction techniques and mitigation strategies.

3 Review the status of existing knowledge, identifying weaknesses or gaps and put forward prioritised proposals for further research.

4 Produce an easily updatable national database of archaeological sites in England where preservation *in situ* schemes involving engineering solutions or redesign have been undertaken.

This study has attempted to draw together the many strands of a development by describing construction processes and their impact on buried archaeological remains, identifying areas in which a more cooperative working method could be more cost-effective, and outlining the most prominent methods by which archaeological remains are currently preserved *in situ*. It has attempted to provide relevant information to all members of a development project without presenting an over-bias in favour of any single profession. However, the three professional backgrounds of the research team are evident in different sections of the text and, as should be the case in any development project, hopefully combine positively in a product that shared a joint aim – here to elucidate the nature, perceived effects and mitigation of construction processes on *in situ* archaeological remains.

1.2 Report structure and contributors

In this section, a definition is given for the types of archaeological sites on which preservation *in situ* may be an issue. The importance of characterising the burial environment of the site is discussed, as this is viewed as a necessary step in the development of mitigation strategies to reduce construction impacts. The role of archaeologists and engineers, and their part in developing mitigation strategies at an early stage is outlined.

Section 2.0 summarises the range of engineering operations that may be employed during a construction project which can impact upon the burial environment of a site and any archaeological remains present. Mitigation options for reducing the impact from individual engineering operations are given. This section is aimed at professionals who advise on or design mitigation strategies – for example planners, architects, developers, statutory undertakers, curators and archaeologists. In this respect, a technical appendix (Appendix A) is provided which includes detailed descriptions of each engineering operation, an assessment of their potential impact on *in situ* remains, and mitigation options to avoid or minimise the impact. In addition to this technical appendix, a summary of the planning framework and operational methodologies that can be used to control development and promote protection of the physical environment is given in Appendix B. An example of a mitigation strategy concerning a site in York is documented in Appendix C for reference purposes.

Section 3.0 presents a review of existing literature, providing further relevant information on the minimisation of construction impacts. A brief discussion of the identified gaps and weaknesses in current knowledge, and research proposals to address these gaps, is given. An annotated bibliography prepared from the literature review is presented in Appendix D, together with a list of the sources consulted.

The final section of this volume, Section 4.0, summarises the results of the study and its conclusions. The summary also describes various mitigation strategies that may be appropriate for inclusion within a development project in order to avoid or reduce construction impact and so permit preservation *in situ* of archaeological remains.

As a separate component of the study, further information on mitigation strategies has been obtained from an assessment of information concerning archaeologically important sites within England which may have been subjected to some form of development activity. This has been facilitated by the production of an easily updatable national database of archaeological sites in England where archaeological mitigation strategies, excluding archaeological excavation, have been undertaken in order to achieve the required preservation *in situ* of the remains present. The database is supplied on a separate CD-ROM, with supporting documentation included in Volume 2 of this report. The documentation includes details of the method of data collection (eg postal questionnaire) and organisations contacted, the database design and a summary of the compiled data.

This requirement of the study to consider both the engineering and archaeological components of a construction project has been made possible because of the multifunctional nature of the research team. Led by Hunting Technical Services (formally Hunting Land & Environment) and Cambridge Archaeological Unit, specialist input has been given by Dr C French from University of Cambridge Archaeology Department and Mr R Thorne from Alan Baxter & Associates Consulting Engineers.

Significant contributions have also been received from a wide range of individuals, many of whom represent the end users of this study (a full list of the individuals and organisations is given in the acknowledgements of this report).

The majority of archaeological and engineering terms used throughout this report are defined at appropriate points within the text and also in a glossary of terms which is included at the rear of the report.

1.3 Archaeological site composition

1.3.1 What constitutes an 'archaeological site'?

Within the discipline of archaeology, the definition of the term 'site' has generated much debate (Hodder and Orton 1976; Schiffer and Gummerman 1977; Gaffney and Tingle 1984; Ingold 1993). As a broad definition, a site can be described as a place in which a particular human event occurred (Kent 1984), a locus of past human behaviour or of cultural remains (Schiffer and Gummerman 1977, 183). Such evidence can include: traces of pits or hearths, or concentrations of artefacts relating to domestic, industrial or spiritual activity; extensive land-organisation features (eg field systems and their internal structures); or more tangible remains of partially preserved historic buildings with attendant yards.

For the purposes of this study, an archaeological site is taken to be an assortment of components or remains (artefacts, deposits, structural and environmental remains) and the individual contexts (burial environments) within which they occur in combination. Their preliminary physical evaluation will indicate their character and survival in terms of preservation/condition (ie whether disturbed/truncated by later events and the extent to which post-depositional factors have had an effect on their physical composition) and in spatial terms, allowing for a clear demonstration of the integrity of the archaeological site. Archaeological mitigation strategies aim to ensure the continued preservation *in situ* of sites which are threatened with destruction during the course of development.

As a below-ground archaeological resource, the remains are held within naturally accreted deposits, or those derived from past occupation surfaces. For example, in the urban environment, the usually deep sequence of sediment or deposit build-up is commonly referred to in geotechnical reports as 'made ground' and is entirely the product of past settlement activity, comprising building and rebuilding events, dumping and quarrying, pit and drain digging, etc. This 'made ground', and often the more consolidated underlying deposits which may be described separately in geotechnical reports, form the archaeological resource. While the top of the natural substratum may define the limits of vertical stratigraphy, cultural remains may intrude into the top of the natural geological sequence in the form of cut features – pits, ditches, graves, basements/cellars, etc. In rural areas, archaeological sites are frequently highly truncated by centuries of ploughing and agricultural activities. While they may have lost a vertical dimension, their survival as cut features is of importance, together with the survival of any buried soils of the former occupation horizon.

1.3.2 Understanding the burial environment

There has often been a common misconception that artefact-conservation research, which describes the 'state of equilibrium' that individual artefacts reach within their immediate environment, has formed the basis of arguments concerned with the preservation of archaeological remains (Dowman 1970; Cronyn 1990). This assumes that it is possible, or even useful, to maintain their preservation in place. Instead, such arguments ignore the composition of the *whole* site area which not only comprises artefacts, deposits and structures, but also the microscopic environmental, faunal or industrial information that combines to provide a more complete and specific site history able to indicate aspects of the local economy, environment or past land-use changes (Schiffer 1987). Since all these individual contexts and contents deteriorate at different rates – rates which accelerate or slow down following interruptive events (eg a construction impact causing dewatering) – the

process of deliberate preservation should take into consideration the value of the site as a whole. That is, the site's *significance* within its local, regional, national and international framework, and what might be considered to be the acceptable loss of various aspects of its composition at the expense of preserving the perceived important site components.

More specifically, and from a curatorial point of view, an understanding of the transformation processes on the diverse archaeological remains present will be of crucial importance if the site is to be managed effectively (Schiffer 1987). Immediately following burial and before further potential transformations caused by impacts from later intrusive activities, the physical, chemical and biological composition of the archaeological remains will have changed in response to the immediate burial environment (Thorne et al 1987). Important scientific information regarding the agents of archaeological deterioration or preservation has come from the few monitoring schemes currently in place on selected archaeological sites (eg Carrott et al 1996), but the results of long-term research into the effects of construction activities is needed before more definitive statements on preservation methods can be made. This is essential in order to predict accurately the effects of proposed preservation schemes. Though at present the burial environment and the processes associated with it are poorly understood, three useful papers on the physical, chemical and biological nature of the burial environment in archaeological sites have been published by Simpson, Pollard and Hopkins in the proceedings of the 1996 conference on *Preserving archaeological remains* in situ (Corfield et al 1998). In addition, efforts have been made to develop generic, quantitative site-decay models; for example, several 'decay and preservation matrices' have been devised which relate the effect of different decay processes to a range of archaeological remains (eg Mathewson and Gonzalez 1988). Though useful to some extent, they have proven to be limited to site-specific cases and cannot be applied as a rule of thumb. This is being addressed partly by work to classify the 'soil archive' with regard to the corrosion of metal artefacts (Wagner et al 1997), and it is hoped bone (Millard 1998). Though the classification scheme is still being developed it will hopefully consider the following important site conditions: the redox chemistry of water within the burial environment (aerobic or anaerobic); whether the burial environment is dry or waterlogged; the diffusion of gases in the deposits; the type of deposits (eg soil characteristics); the chemical composition of the groundwater; and the level of microbial activity.

A successful mitigation strategy will therefore be reliant on: identifying both the proposed construction impacts and the type and character of the remains present; assessing the existing state of preservation of the remains; and understanding the surrounding burial environment and its past sequence of change. The most important starting point for the preservation strategy must be with the professional archaeological site-evaluation report, which should determine the character, nature, date, state of preservation and significance of the site remains (cf Institute of Field Archaeologists 1994: *Standard and guidance for archaeological field evaluations*). Additional information on the burial environment of a site may be obtained by reference to geotechnical reports prepared following ground and contamination investigations. It may, however, be necessary to obtain further archaeological information on the burial environment, and this can be undertaken following an assessment of the likely construction impacts that will be caused during the site's development. Descriptions of typically used construction operations, their potential construction impact on *in situ* remains, and mitigation options to reduce their impact are discussed in Section 2.0.

1.4 Summarising the archaeological framework and the development team

In 1992 the revised European Convention on the Protection of the Archaeological Heritage was signed by representatives of 20 member states of the Council of Europe. It was accompanied by the 1990 Charter for the Protection and Management of the Archaeological Heritage, which sets out the principles and guidelines to preserve *in situ* or by record archaeological remains found either in research or in development projects (cf *Antiquity* 1993: Special Section on Archaeological heritage management). This Charter and its Convention endorsed in the remit of PPG 16 (DoE 1990), coupled with *Management of archaeological projects* (English Heritage 1990; its revision in 1991 now commonly known as MAP 2), brought about a revolution in the concept, planning and management of archaeological projects of all kinds. The Charter was directed at local and central government planning authorities and developers, with the aim of producing common links and routes to achieve a successful balance between development or research work and the preservation of the archaeological heritage. (The planning framework in England and current legislation relevant to archaeological sites are summarised in Appendix B.)

Written for an international agenda, the guidelines of the Charter are designed to be incorporated into national/regional agendas and structure plans in ways that presiding officers consider appropriate. Article 3 of the Charter (Legislation and economy) presents a clear acknowledgement of the vulnerability of the archaeological resource and the need for its protection:

The protection of the archaeological heritage should be considered as a moral obligation upon all human beings; it is also a collective public responsibility. This obligation must be acknowledged through relevant legislation and the provision of adequate funds for the supporting programmes necessary for efficient heritage management.

Similarly, within PPG 16:

Archaeological remains should be seen as a finite and non-renewable resource [Paragraph 6, and] Where nationally important remains, whether scheduled or not, and their settings, are affected by proposed development there should be a presumption in favour of their physical preservation [Paragraph 8].

With the adoption of the Charter and the publication of PPG 16, the process for preserving archaeological remains *in situ* as part of a mitigation strategy for a development, has become a necessary and logical part of the management repertoire of archaeological curators in England. However, in seeking to conform to the requirements of PPG 16, developers are often confounded at the outset of their projects by the current paucity of detailed archaeological information in public databases that could assist in delimiting areas of significant or known archaeology, and initiate the early use of avoidance measures. In response to this problem, a programme to review and synthesise the current state of England's historic towns, comprising urban archaeological assessments, databases and strategy documents, has been initiated by English Heritage (English Heritage 1992). The development of archaeological GIS programmes, supported by detailed gazetteer information and the definition of zones of archaeological importance and/or of development restriction, will facilitate the planning and management of the archaeological heritage (in these selected urban areas at least), thus reducing the conflicts of interest between 'the need to preserve nationally important archaeological remains and the need to allow our towns to thrive and develop' (Wainwright 1993, 418).

Aside from the obvious benefits of international and national guidance policies, there remain a number of grey areas in the planning of development projects that beset the coexistence of archaeology and the construction industry. For instance, a major concern to the archaeological community is the incorporation of advice and/or evaluation fieldwork at a suitably early stage in a development project. Conversely, a developer may not be familiar with the roles of different archaeological personnel and thus the appropriate lines of communication which enable the effective incorporation of archaeological considerations into the project's design stage and construction programme.

As will be evident in the following sections, it is without doubt that the evaluation of archaeological 'problems' during the early stages of development work result in a more cost-effective construction programme in which archaeologically sympathetic redesigns or modifications enable a more direct and trouble-free path to development completion than might otherwise be the case. Therefore, the successful design, installation and maintenance of an archaeological mitigation strategy is achieved through good communication between the developer, engineer, the archaeologist and the main contractor team. Consideration of a site's sensitivity and an integrated mitigation strategy should unite all the development stages.

Economic considerations should also unite all professionals involved because the cost of change increases greatly during a project, such that the unplanned incorporation of an engineered mitigation strategy into the construction phase of a project may be financially disastrous (as demonstrated in Figure 1). For example, massive cost over-runs occurred on the Rose Theatre site in London, where the developer spent an estimated £11 million funding both a six-month excavation and subsequent alterations to their building design (Ove Arup 1991).

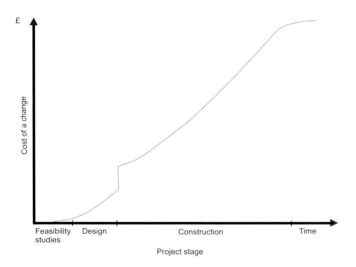

Figure 1 Cost of change against project stage (After Institution of Civil Engineers 1996)

Traditionally advice from archaeologists was reactive, and sought by an engineer if the site either contained known archaeological remains, or if remains were unexpectedly discovered during the development. In this situation, an archaeologist may have been asked to carry out a specific task, for example to seek statutory consents if protected archaeological monuments were affected by the development, or undertake assessment, evaluations, watching briefs, etc. A simplified view of this approach is given in Figure 2, where the promoter of a project (ie developer) employs a consulting engineer to design the project and a contractor to carry out its construction. The project has been divided into an 'initiation', 'design' and 'construction' phase and, although archaeological involvement is not specifically identified, the archaeologists and other specialist contractors would be brought in by the engineer or promoter as and when specific tasks were required of them.

However, the success of a development in integrating with the surrounding natural and built environment, and the acceptability of the way in which it modifies and impacts on

it, cannot be ensured wholly by planning regulations and procedures. Therefore, the avoidance of all construction activities that may impact on archaeological remains requires archaeological advice to be sought during the initial planning of a project; that is, before the submission of development proposals to a planning authority. Though specifically for London, guidance on the procedures for seeking such archaeological advice and the development of mitigation strategies to achieve preservation *in situ* in advance of gaining planning permission has been revised by the Greater London Archaeology Advisory Service (English Heritage 1995, reissued 1998). Following the initiation and design phase, it must not be forgotten that further archaeological advice is also likely to be required during construction of the development, for example in order that any planning constraints are observed and the unforeseen is allowed for.

A revision to the example shown in Figure 2 is therefore suggested to include consultation with an archaeological organisation or consultant during each phase of a development project. This revision is shown in Figure 3 and, although it will not apply to all development projects because it assumes a high level of archaeological sensitivity, this example is a useful indicator of the communication route of achieving preservation *in situ* of a site's archaeological remains. Using the example given by Figure 3, the improved approach to communication could prevent the problem where potential construction impacts identified by an archaeologist may not have been communicated effectively by the engineer to the promoter, possibly because of a reluctance to inform them of unanticipated increased archaeological costs. This failure in communication could result in an inadequate or inappropriate mitigation strategy being adopted that could compromise the objective of achieving continuing archaeological preservation *in situ*, or alternatively, it could result in the costly need to revise the mitigation strategy once the project has started.

Figure 3 stresses the key objective of the early consideration of a site's archaeological resource. This may be achieved in some cases if an Environmental Impact Assessment (EIA) is carried out in advance of obtaining the planning consent for a development to proceed. The regulations for an EIA recommend that a description be included of a site's 'historic heritage, archaeological sites and features', and that the description should include the 'effects of the development on buildings, the architectural and historic heritage, archaeological features, and other human artefacts' (DoE 1989). Depending on a site's relative significance, the production of this description should raise the issue of preservation *in situ*, as detailed in PPG 16, and the need for a mitigation strategy to avoid damage to the archaeological remains by the proposed development. A further benefit of conducting an EIA is that it would usually be produced by a multidisciplinary team of professionals, which might include, among others, planners, engineers, archaeologists and environmentalists.

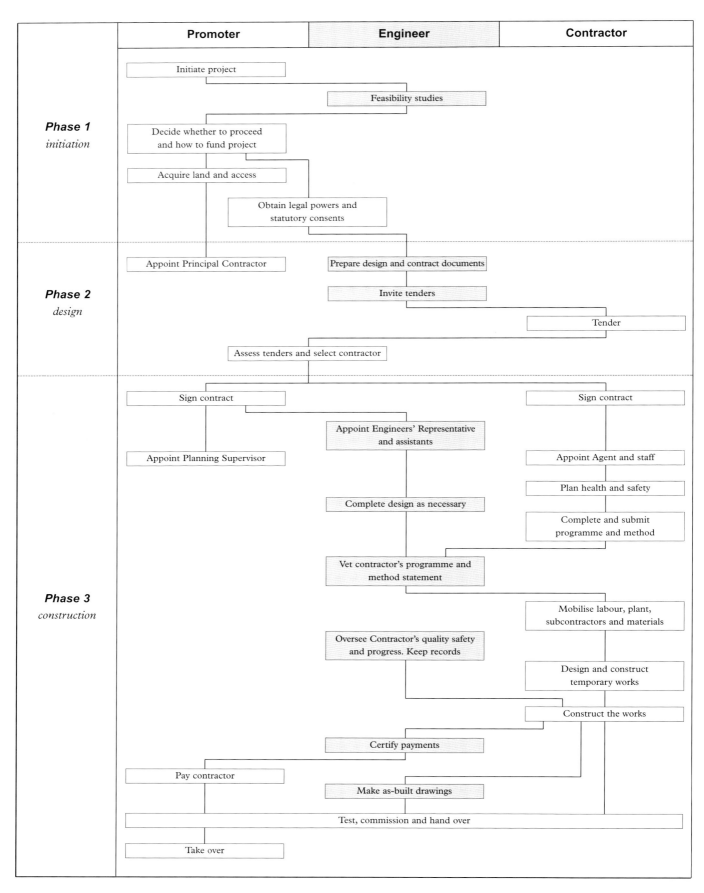

Figure 2 Flow chart showing activities of promoter, engineer and contractor (Source: Institution of Civil Engineers 1996)

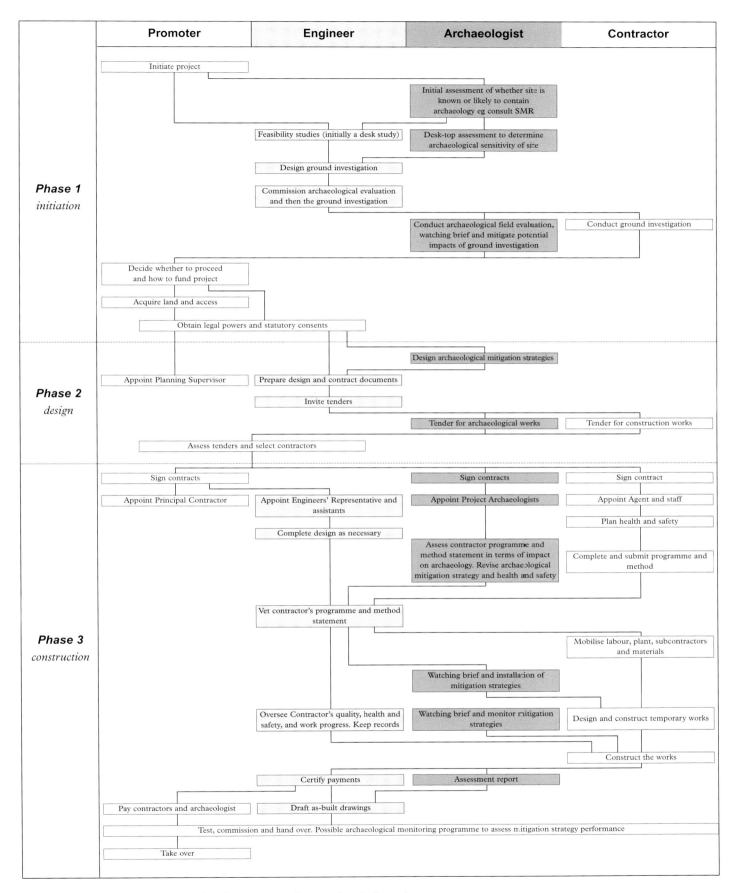

Figure 3 Flow chart showing activities of promoter, engineer, archaeologist and contractor

Though not individually specified at each of the three project phases shown in Figure 3, the archaeological involvement in the planning process can be divided into two or sometimes three roles:

1   Archaeological Curator – who is responsible for the care of a region's archaeological resource through the administration of relevant legislation, the implementation of policies and ensuring that an archaeological programme of investigation and analysis is completed (often through to full publication). Such curators are Development Control Officers, based in County Council Planning or Heritage/ Leisure departments, and are not to be confused with museum curators.

2   Archaeological Contractor – a professional archaeological company or individual, employed to carry out different types of archaeological fieldwork, recording and analysis of the investigated resource. The archaeological contractor will identify the need for further work, and supply relevant quantifiable information to this end in a desk-top or evaluation report to assist the curator in making an informed judgement and recommendations for further work, if necessary.

3   Archaeological Consultant – a professional archaeologist hired by a developer at the outset of a development project, to advise on the type of field and post-excavation commitment, secure all the necessary consents, hire an archaeological contractor on behalf of the developer through a tendering process, and liaise with the local archaeological curator regarding the method and objectives of such work. Archaeological consultants will ensure that the archaeological resource is a considered and well-accommodated aspect of the development programme in line with PPG 16, while maintaining the developer's financial interests.

The provision of specialist advice on various aspects of the project, eg artefact/environmental preservation or mitigation strategy options, may also be sought from other archaeological/geotechnical specialists, or directly from the English Heritage Regional Inspector or Archaeological Science Advisor.

In addition to the above archaeological professionals, the key individuals in the initiation and construction of the development are:

1   Promoter – the initiator of a civil-engineering/development project, eg site owner or developer.

2   Architect – commissioned by the promoter to provide the structural design of the development.

3   Consulting Engineer – a chartered engineer who is approached by an architect, promoter or another engineer for the purpose of designing a building or road, etc.

4   Resident Engineer – a civil engineer who watches the interests of the promoter at a site, working under the consulting engineer.

5   Geotechnical Engineer – an engineer who specialises in rock mechanics, soil mechanics, foundations, groundwater, etc.

6   Main Contractor – a contracting company commissioned to undertake specified work within a defined timescale. The main contractor of a project will conduct most of the tasks concerned with the various stages of the development project.

7   Subcontractor – an organisation hired to undertake specialist work for a main contractor (eg piling crew, landscapers, etc).

2.0 ENGINEERING OPERATIONS

2.1 Introduction

The development of a site generally comprises four stages of construction activity, each of which will involve a wide variety of potentially ground-disturbing (archaeologically damaging) engineering operations. The engineering operations considered in this study are those primarily associated with construction projects that add to, or renew, the existing stock of buildings or roads within England.

The four stages of construction activity, including the main engineering operations which can impact on archaeological remains, are listed below:

Stage 1: Pre-construction ground investigation
This usually commences with a desk-top study which collates all relevant site-specific data. A geotechnical and geochemical ground investigation usually follows which can involve ground-intrusive engineering operations that may result in damage to any buried archaeological remains.

Stage 2: Pre-construction activities
This stage comprises engineering operations that are concerned with making a site ready for construction. Though they vary greatly from site to site, they generally serve to secure the site, remove unwanted obstructions, stabilise the ground and create the necessary infrastructure for construction to proceed. There is often widespread or localised disturbance of the ground during this stage.

Stage 3: Construction activities
This stage includes all the activities associated with the construction of a development, and the main potential impact on archaeological remains usually results from groundwork operations (ie foundations and installation of buried services, or construction of earthworks).

Stage 4: Post-construction remedial and maintenance activities
This includes the various construction activities associated with the repair, maintenance and improvement of a development. Since these activities can involve ground-intrusive engineering operations there is a risk that archaeological remains may be adversely affected.

The engineering operations used during these four stages of a development are summarised in the following four sections of this report (Section 2.2 to 2.5) and are detailed more fully in Appendix A.

Appendix A has been structured in accordance with these four stages, and each engineering operation is detailed under the stage where it first typically occurs in the construction programme. For each operation, there is a description of its purpose or function to an engineer, the equipment (plant) required, the frequency of its use, the disturbance it may cause to near-surface soils, and the mitigation options that might be employed to avoid or minimise that disturbance.

Though the physical, chemical and biological decay processes and their interrelationships in a burial environment are complex, the impact that various engineering operations have on these processes must be considered when discussing the ground disturbance they can cause. Particular attention has been paid to disturbances that result in physical movement (excavation, displacement, compaction, heave and stresses, etc) and water-regime changes (retention or exclusion, flow patterns and rates, quality and temperature, etc). This is because it is these two parameters which are thought to change most significantly the character of the burial environment. For example, ground movement can physically damage archaeological remains, physically move the remains and so alter their site context, and structurally alter the deposits in which the remains are preserved. Impact on archaeological remains by the absence or presence of water can be physical (eg abrasion, solution and volume changes), chemical (eg universal catalyst and an electrolyte) and/or biological (eg favours anaerobic or aerobic microbial populations) (Thompson 1997). In summary, the chemical interaction between the burial environment and the archaeological remains it contains is mediated largely by the quantity and chemical nature of water present, either as the soil solution occurring above the water table or the groundwater below it (Pollard 1998). The soil solution and groundwater are the water held within the soil matrix and the dissolved load it contains (ie concentration of soluble salts, ions, etc). Though regularly reported, it is worth repeating that in England the presence on a site of waterlogged and anaerobic burial conditions often gives the greatest preservation of organic artefacts and environmental remains.

2.2 Stage 1: Pre-construction ground investigation

2.2.1 Introduction and design of a ground investigation

The pre-construction ground investigation generally commences with a desk-top study in which documented information relating to the site chosen for development and its immediate vicinity is compiled and evaluated. This is followed by a ground investigation which typically involves engineering operations that cause ground disturbance and so impact on archaeological remains *in situ*. The investigation is most likely to be carried out by a specialist geotechnical engineer who would usually conduct the investigation in accordance with British Standards Institution's *Code of practice for site investigations* (BS 5930: 1999). For those previously developed sites that may be contaminated, the ground investigation is also likely to involve a geochemical specialist, who may make reference to British Standards Institution's *Code of practice: the investigation of potentially contaminated sites* (BS 10175: 2001).

In summary, the engineer would ideally adhere to the following sequence of work:

1 thorough preliminary desk study
2 air-photograph interpretation
3 walkover survey
4 first stage of ground investigation
5 interpretation of geology and characterisation of the strata from laboratory tests
6 further ground investigation of areas of interest or confusion identified in the first stage
7 full programme of laboratory testing for both geotechnical and contamination assessment
8 evaluation of all available data
9 derivation of design parameters and preparation of a comprehensive geotechnical report

However, many small site investigations may be severely limited by budget constraints, or be designed by non-specialists who are interested in specifics rather than a comprehensive picture of the site. A particular risk in this case is the omission of the desk study, or at best the investigation may be condensed to the following stages:

1 basic desk study
2 walkover survey
3 single-stage ground investigation
4 full programme of laboratory testing for both geotechnical and contamination assessment
5 evaluation of available data

6 derivation of design parameters and preparation of a geotechnical report

The desk study involves the compilation of all the available relevant information about the site that can be obtained without sampling or testing. The type of site information to be compiled includes topography, geology, hydrogeology, hydrology, previous uses, restrictions on development (legislative or practical), geotechnical problems and environmental constraints (eg archaeological and ecological).

During a walkover survey, the lie of the land will be ascertained, primarily to determine suitable access routes for equipment to be used during the ground investigation, but also to gain visible evidence relating to the above types of information.

Having completed the desk study and walkover survey, a programme of ground investigation may then be required. From an engineering perspective the purpose of a ground investigation is to obtain a comprehensive picture of the engineering behaviour of soils or rocks at a site to permit the safe, economical and acceptable design of a proposed development. The chemical nature of the soils and rocks is also assessed insofar as it poses a risk to harm or pollute the environment. For example, substances in the soil could impact on the longevity of buried building materials, cause pollution of nearby water bodies, and affect the health and safety of construction workers. The design will therefore include numbers and locations of sampling points, and the methods of excavation and sample collection. The number and locations and depths of exploratory holes carried out as part of a ground investigation are usually governed by the available budget, site access, ground conditions and perhaps the available time. There are no published rules for the location of exploratory excavations, other than general guidance which stipulates that the required sampling density increases with the complexity of building design and geological conditions. As a guide, the following three examples of construction projects give an idea of likely spacing of exploratory holes.

1 **A small urban site of uniform geology on which a simple medium-rise structure is to be erected**
   A borehole is required in each corner of the site and one or two in the middle. If the spacing between boreholes so situated is significantly more than 40–50m then more exploratory holes (ie boreholes or static cone penetration tests) are introduced in order to achieve this magnitude of spacing. Trial pits tend to be situated independently of the deep excavations on such a site and are more frequent, perhaps being spaced 25m apart. This is due both to the usual greater variability of near-surface soils and the lesser cost of trial pits. If these excavations reveal more complicated ground conditions than supposed then further investigation is required.

2   **A small but sensitive urban site of uniform geology on which a complicated structure is to be erected**
Boreholes located at a spacing of 20m across the footprint of the structure, with trial pits at a similar spacing.

3   **Road construction**
A borehole at the site of each bridge foundation and alternate boreholes and trial pits at 100m intervals along the road line. Boreholes are preferred at sites of embankments and cuttings. Trial pits should not be excavated below the proposed road pavement or foundation levels.

Though limited guidance is given by the current British Standards' *Code of practice for site investigations*, it does give a single recommendation that a 10–30m spacing of exploratory holes is appropriate for structures (BS 5930: 1999). There is also guidance available for the investigation of contaminated sites, in which the number and distribution of sampling points are prescribed in order to maximise the likelihood of encountering 'hot spots' of contamination (BS 10175: 2001). For example, if based on a regular grid pattern the recommended minimum number of sampling points for a site 1.0 or 5.0 hectares in size is 25 and 85 respectively.

More detailed guidance is given for the depth of investigation, and normally the exploratory holes should be taken to below all deposits that may be unsuitable for foundations purposes (BS 5930: 1999). Such a requirement can create a high risk of ground-investigation techniques impacting on *in situ* archaeological remains, since the remains are typically located in the near-surface deposits of 'made ground' or weak compressible soils.

The importance of a ground investigation must not be underestimated because it is prerequisite to the safe and economical design of the final development. From a planning perspective, the information will assist developers and engineers in determining which engineering operations, for example foundation design, will be both environmentally and archaeologically acceptable for use at the site. To eliminate the ground investigation, which usually ranges from about 0.5–1.0 per cent of total construction costs, only to find that major redesigns are necessary after construction has started is a false economy (Bowles 1996). This fact is generally recognised for geotechnical issues, but perhaps it is less well appreciated for assessing archaeological issues.

2.2.2 Engineering operations used during a ground investigation

When a ground investigation is undertaken it generally involves a combination of engineering operations that broadly fit into the following four categories:

1   Boring, excavation and sampling involving the breaking, digging and removal of soil or rock.
2   Probing involving the pushing or driving of a rigid, often instrumented probe into the ground.
3   Techniques and tests in preformed boreholes.
4   Geophysical surveying using techniques that map variations in the earth's elastic or electrical properties, or gravitational and magnetic fields.

Although the main focus in this section is on ground investigation for buildings and other structures where the cost per unit area is high (eg a compact urban site), many of the engineering operations described are also applicable to roads, airfields, pipelines, power lines and other extended sites.

The most widely used method of ground investigation is boring holes into the ground, from which *in situ* tests may be conducted or samples are collected for either visual inspection or laboratory testing. Hand augers and trial pits are typically used for shallow-ground investigations, while ground conditions at greater depths are investigated using shafts or boreholes. The most common methods of investigation and the variety of *in situ* tests available for use by the engineer are described in BS 5930 *Code of practice for site investigations* (BS 5930: 1999). Two examples of ground-investigation techniques which illustrate the difference in scale of operation are shown on Figures 4 and 5.

Figure 4   Light cable percussion boring at a rural location in Cambridgeshire (Photo: Hunting Technical Services)

Figure 5 'Window sampler' boring at an urban location in Yorkshire (Photo: Hunting Technical Services)

Ground-investigation techniques involving probing chiefly comprise dynamic or static cone penetration tests. The tests provide the engineer with information on ground conditions by the ease with which a cone can be pushed or driven into the ground, and depths of 20m or more can be achieved with the cone.

Ground-investigation techniques in preformed boreholes include a variety of tests that generally provide information on physical soil parameters; for example, a field vane determines the undrained strength of the soil. Tests may also involve the introduction or removal of water from an excavation in order to assess the ground's permeability.

Geophysical surveying techniques are used to measure variations in physical properties of the ground. Common methods used include electrical resistivity, ground-penetrating radar and seismic methods. These different techniques generally operate by locating anomalies in the buried soil profile, for example saturated and unsaturated materials, and buried features, possibly of archaeological interest.

2.2.3 Impact of engineering operations used during a ground investigation

Boring and excavation operations will result in severe disturbance of the ground and the potential loss of much important archaeological information. Within the excavated area the impact on archaeological remains must be viewed as the total loss of material, unless the remains had previously been excavated and preserved by 'record'.

Though at times less obvious, engineering operations involving excavation may also cause an impact on remains located outside the excavated area. For example, if surface loading by an excavator applies a pressure greater than the underlying soil strength then the soil will fail by shearing (physically moving the soil and archaeological remains). In addition, even if the strength of the soil is sufficient to carry the applied pressure, ground compaction is still likely under such conditions which will cause the soil particles to move closer together and the soil layers to become thinner as the air content is reduced. Physical damage to archaeological remains and a change to the surrounding burial environment may occur and therefore, in terms of the *in situ* preservation, it is normally desirable to avoid compaction and reduce the incidence of shear failure wherever possible.

The use of inappropriately sized or designed tools to undertake the excavation can extend the area of ground disturbance, thereby increasing construction impact on archaeological remains. Therefore the correct tools should be selected to create the size of excavation required by the engineer, given the ground conditions present. For example, the bucket width and operating reach of an excavator should be appropriate for the width and depth of trial pit required. The bucket may also need to be 'toothless' to avoid ripping through archaeological layers.

The placement of arisings (spoil) on ground surrounding an excavation may create an impact on archaeological remains *in situ*; for example, it can cause intermixing of the two materials and compaction of the ground due to the imposed load. In addition, on a contaminated site the placement of arisings may introduce potentially aggressive contaminants to the surrounding *in situ* archaeology.

Drilling fluids, borehole casings and other accessory equipment used during the ground investigation may cause a physical, chemical or biological disturbance of the ground. For example, drilling fluids may comprise water, air, mud and foam, and the introduction of any one of these into undisturbed ground may adversely affect the continuing preservation *in situ* of archaeological remains.

Many ground-investigation techniques which involve tests in preformed excavations cause little construction impact, once the necessary excavation has been formed (eg borehole or trial pit). However, further ground disturbance may result from the operation of certain tests, for example plate-loading tests that measure stiffness of the ground can cause ground movement through compaction. If a test involves the introduction or removal of water (eg permeability tests), this can adversely affect the burial environment surrounding archaeological remains. For example, the change may be physical (increase or decrease soil-moisture content), chemical (mobilise insoluble salts in the soil) or biological (introduce polluted water).

Though rarely used as a sole means of ground investigation, geophysical surveying techniques are predominately non-invasive as they require contact with the ground surface only, and therefore they are unlikely to impact on buried archaeological remains. Geophysical techniques which require the provision of a preformed borehole will not in themselves cause an impact on the buried archaeology, since the only stage of ground disturbance is in formation of the borehole.

2.2.4 Mitigation of impact from engineering operations used during a ground investigation

In major development projects, prior to conducting a full desktop study and ground investigation, there generally occurs a lengthy and detailed process of site assessment. If possible this should include a consideration of the potential construction impacts and mitigation options; these can then be explored in detail during the desk study.

The importance being attached to the archaeological resource is justified because it can act as a serious constraint on the completion of a development project and, in most site assessments, it is the financial viability of a project that is a promoter's first and foremost consideration. The early analysis of a site's archaeological importance will also assist in the eventual preparation of a planning application because archaeological remains are accepted as a material consideration in determining planning applications (DoE 1990).

Assuming that the site assessment concludes that a development project is viable, the developer or promoter (project's fund-raiser) may then commission both archaeological and engineering desk-top studies.

From an archaeological perspective, a desk-top study will provide and discuss evidence for the archaeology of a site in terms of local, regional or national importance and suggest the nature of further work necessary to mitigate the impact of development (DoE 1990; IFA 1994, rev 2001). By this early stage of a project the formal opinion of an archaeologist should therefore have been sought, and this view is given in the British Standards Institution's *Code of practice for site investigations* which states that: 'should it become apparent during a desk-top study that any ancient monument or site of archaeological interest is likely to be affected by the [ground] investigation or the subsequent works, the matter should be referred to the Chief Inspector of Ancient Monuments' (BS 5930: 1999).

The presence of archaeological remains on or adjacent to a site can impose a serious financial or practical constraint on a development project. It is therefore desirable to comprehend the scale of this constraint and build appropriate 'safety nets' into the design at the earliest possible stage. Even though the nature or type of archaeological remains that may be present will not be fully known during the design stage, the engineering operations that are envisaged in the development may be critically assessed in terms of their potential impact on *in situ*

archaeological remains. The outline construction method generated during this stage will be of immense importance to the archaeologist in defining areas of high, moderate or low archaeological sensitivity to construction impacts. It will also assist in suggesting either that alternative engineering operations should be used, or that further archaeological involvement be incorporated in order to implement a mitigation strategy.

If this advice, which is commonly provided by local or national government archaeological development control officers or by consultants, occurs at a sufficiently early stage in the design of a project, it can be successfully used by the design team to deflect many of the construction impacts away from areas of suspected archaeological sensitivity.

Since there are various suites of data from a desk-top study which are of mutual benefit to both engineers and archaeologists, it is recommended that data collection be coordinated between the various professional disciplines. If this is achieved it can avoid duplication of effort and improve data consistency. It is also financially desirable since both engineer and archaeologist are generally funded by the same client (ie promoter). A single development team meeting to discuss the requirements of each desk-top contributor could resolve this issue.

Coordination of effort is also important because some areas of data interpretation may not previously have been explored by the development team. For instance, in rural locations aerial-photographic surveys are frequently undertaken to assess the potential for the presence of archaeological sites by interpreting and accurately mapping crop and soil marks. Such features may also provide significant information to engineers concerning varying ground conditions across a site, for example areas of deep soil, wet ground, buried constructions (eg pipelines and former airstrips) and unstable ground (eg backfilled excavations).

Following the desk-top study, a ground investigation may be undertaken by both the engineer and archaeologist. Again, to maximise the information retrieved from a ground investigation and minimise impact on the archaeology present, coordination between the two disciplines should be aimed for.

An example of the usefulness of coordinated data collection is during the geotechnical borehole surveys. These generally exclude detail and description of the uppermost part of the soil profile, which is usually classified simply as 'overburden' or 'made ground'. In rural environments this overburden can constitute the entire 'positive' archaeological zone (eg surviving buried soil layers). In urban environments, it may consist mostly of modern surface layers but also include a significant proportion of the upper stratigraphic profile of an archaeological sequence. Adequate recording by an archaeologist of this horizon during a standard borehole survey may provide a useful insight into the absence or presence of archaeological remains and their surrounding burial environment.

Alternatively, consideration could be given to the greater standardisation of the logging of borehole cores and soil profiles. For example, within the UK a method description is given by the British Standards' *Code of practice for site investigations* (BS 5930: 1999). Though aspects of this method of describing ground conditions may be familiar to archaeologists, it is likely that areas of confusion could arise in its direct application to archaeological deposits, such as description of deposit colour and consistency. The possibility for such confusion must be recognised because it could have implications for the design and eventual adoption of a mitigation strategy during construction of a new development.

The trial pits and boreholes of the ground investigation are probably of greatest concern and also interest to an archaeologist. Both form a major component of most ground investigations and when dug they create total ground disturbance within the area of excavation. This construction impact can be exacerbated if inappropriate or poorly maintained equipment is used to form the excavation, or the operator is insufficiently trained in use of the equipment and has not been made aware of the archaeological sensitivity of a site. Accurate site plans showing the location of the trial pits and boreholes, which may also be marked out on the ground, and supervision of their excavation will again mitigate against uncontrolled construction impacts. Rutting and compaction of the adjacent ground surface by equipment may also occur during the ground investigation. These impacts can be mitigated by: carefully planning to avoid areas of archaeological sensitivity; ensuring the work is conducted by trained operators who may also be under archaeological supervision; and confirmation that the correct equipment is used to form the excavation. The timing of operations to avoid inappropriate weather conditions is also an important consideration, particularly when the soil is wet and has poor strength. The degree of ground disturbance can be lessened by reducing the pressures applied to it and/or increasing its soil strength. This may be achieved by adapting the equipment used (eg load-spreading plates and low-pressure tyres on an excavator) and by protecting the ground surface on which the equipment operates (eg using a geotextile mat). The use of geotextiles and other temporary working surfaces is an important consideration as they act as a buffer between surface operations and *in situ* archaeological remains, thus increasing soil strength. Their use may be to spread loads, prevent surface rutting and avoid contamination of the ground by drilling muds or other fluids.

Following completion of a ground investigation, the backfilling of excavations must be conducted with due consideration of the *in situ* archaeology. Ideally, backfill should recreate as closely as possible the ground conditions that existed before the excavation. Replacement of excavated arisings should be undertaken in the correct sequence of removal and be conducted in a controlled manner. If the arisings are unsuitable (eg contaminated) or difficult to handle (eg stiff clay), then an imported material may be necessary to complete the backfill to the satisfaction of both the engineer and archaeologist. The correct selection and handling of an engineered backfill material for a mitigation strategy is of utmost importance, for which expert

technical advice may be required. The literature review, detailed in Appendix D, revealed that the selection and use of various backfill materials on archaeological sites have been researched extensively in America (eg US Army Engineer Waterways Experiment Station 1992) but that only limited examples are available in England (eg Canti 1995).

2.3 Stage 2: Pre-construction activities

2.3.1 Engineering operations used during pre-construction activities

Before construction of the new development can commence a certain amount of site preparation is usually required. Conducted as part of the main construction contract, or let as a separate 'enabling works' contract, the engineering operations used may range from simply clearing away areas of surface vegetation to a major operation involving soil stripping and *in situ* remediation of land contamination. The site-preparation activities also involve mobilisation of personnel and equipment (plant) to be employed on the third and main stage of a construction project.

On a large development project the following engineering operations, that can result in ground disturbance, may be required (Chudley and Greeno 2001):

1 site fencing and hoarding
2 protection of existing features
3 access roads
4 contractor accommodation
5 site storage facilities
6 electricity and water supply and drainage
7 vegetation removal and topsoil stripping
8 remediation of land contamination
9 pile probing
10 demolition and site clearance
11 shoring
12 ground improvement
13 trial piles
14 tower crane bases

The engineering operations listed above are described in detail in Section A2.0 of Appendix A.

Frequently the first operation is to secure the boundaries of the project site, especially as this can be a planning requirement imposed on the developer. Foundations for the fencing will typically require excavations every 1.5–2.0m around the site perimeter, to a depth of around 750mm and a diameter of approximately 300mm. Similar fencing may be required within the site to provide a secure compound for stores, plant or accommodation, or to protect existing features (eg trees) from site activities. Once established, the storage areas and contractor's accommodation (comprising either portable office units or existing buildings) may require the provision of pathways, car-parking areas, services, drains, septic tanks, etc. In addition, access roads may be constructed over the site to facilitate equipment movements.

Heavy plant may be brought on to the site to undertake a range of clearance operations that can include vegetation and soil stripping, demolition and removal of previous structures (eg foundations, storage tanks), and removal of land contamination. For two different but related reasons, the use of heavy plant for site clearance is likely to increase in England. Firstly, within the planning process there is now a clear presumption in favour of the reuse of previously developed land (ie brownfield sites), as opposed to allowing the development to occur on agricultural land (ie greenfield sites). Typically brownfield sites require a greater degree of site clearance to make them suitable for development. Secondly, a new contaminated-land regime was introduced into England on 1 April 2000 (Part IIA of the Environmental Protection Act 1990, inserted by section 57 of the Environment Act 1995). This Part IIA regime will be used as a means of dealing with the legacy of contaminated land which has arisen from the historical use of the land for a wide range of industrial, mining and waste-disposal activities. However, because Part IIA is intended to be complementary to the Planning Regime, and much of England's contaminated land is associated with brownfield sites, it is expected that most contaminated land will continue to be dealt with by use of planning conditions. Further details of the regime are contained in the Department of the Environment, Transport and the Regions (DETR) Circular *Environmental Protection Act 1990: Part IIA Contaminated Land* (DETR 2000). A useful overview of the effects of remediation on the heritage value of the built environment and landscape can be found in an R & D report by the Environment Agency *Assessing the wider environment value of remediating land contamination: a review* (Bardos et al 2000).

If there is a requirement to remediate land contamination (either in solid, liquid or gaseous form) the following approaches may be used (CIRIA 1995a–b):

1 Excavation and disposal of the contaminated material.
2 Containment and isolation of the contaminated ground with in-ground barriers.
3 *In situ* remediation by removing, destroying or modifying contaminants without their prior excavation or extraction.

The engineering operations associated with the first two approaches would be similar to those used during general ground-excavation and groundwater-control operations. Though still relatively uncommon in England, *in situ* remediation methods may rely on physical, chemical, thermal and/or biological processes and so could drastically alter the ground conditions of a site. Examples of the most frequently encountered *in situ* based methods are given by the Environment Agency in *Survey of remedial techniques for land contamination in England and Wales* (Petts et al 2000) and by CIRIA in their series of 12 reports on *Remedial treatment for contaminated land* (CIRIA 1995).

In some cases, especially following the site-clearance operations, the ground may be weak and unsuitable to carry construction plant and foundations. Engineering operations may then remove the weak soils in bulk and replace them with compacted granular material, or the strength of the soil can be increased by using a range of ground-improvement techniques. The methods include surcharging, dynamic compaction, vibro-compaction, vibroreplacement, grouting or deep drainage.

If the site is affected by a high groundwater level, dewatering operations may be employed to both control the groundwater and ensure the stability of excavations and works during construction. Dewatering operations used can include groundwater exclusion (eg sheet piling, grouting, slurry cut-off walls, compressed air and ground freezing), or abstraction methods (eg gravity drains, sumps, wellpoints and electro-osmosis).

Once these works have been completed, preparation for construction can commence. This might include laying a piling platform (eg layer of brick debris), conducting a pile test, constructing a crane base or other similar temporary works.

2.3.2 Impact of engineering operations used during pre-construction activities

During site preparation, shallow ground disturbance may initially be caused by excavations for hoarding and fencing, followed by the laying of services or drains to the site accommodation. Unless existing or overhead service lines are used, this is likely to be carried out using mechanical excavators in the manner of shallow trial trenches dug during the ground investigation.

The potential for shallow but more extensive ground disturbance exists if access roads or storage areas are required across the site. Their construction often involves the removal of soft areas of ground and the laying of a firm granular base. As well as direct physical disturbance this introduces a new material to the site which could be chemically aggressive to near-surface archaeological remains (eg increasing pH due to the use of crushed chalk). The material will also impose a load, so causing possible compaction of the ground. Examples of site-preparation operations where a time constraint and an access restriction can lead to the increased occurrence of ground disturbance are shown on Figures 6 and 7.

Across a site, the most extensive physical impact on buried archaeology may occur during the removal of vegetation, topsoil and buried obstructions. Removal of the surface soil layer also exposes the underlying subsoil to compaction and contamination from machine traffic, and the influence of weather fluctuations (eg desiccation, waterlogging and freezing).

Figure 6 Excessive surface rutting caused by machining in wet ground conditions (King's Dyke Pit, Whittlesey, Cambridgeshire (Photo: Cambridge Archaeological Unit)

If the pre-construction groundwork contract involves a programme of *in situ* remediation of site contamination, the impact on archaeological remains and their surrounding burial environment may be severe. Depending on the remediation approach used, the impact may be physical (eg deep ploughing, soil heat treatment), chemical (eg amelioration of soil pH) or biological (eg introducing new micro-organism or increasing microbial activity).

If work is needed to improve or remediate poor ground conditions by the excavation and replacement of poor soil, the impact on archaeology will be similar to that described for excavations during a ground investigation. Alternatively, ground improvement may be conducted *in situ*, for example increasing the soil's strength by placing a load (surcharging) or dropping a weight (dynamic compaction) on to the ground surface, or by inserting a vibrating poker into the ground to improve the soil's strength (vibrocompaction). Ground improvement may also introduce a foreign material to increase the overall *in situ* strength of the soil, for example stone can be introduced at the same time as the vibrating poker to produce stone columns (vibroplacement). Physical disturbance of the ground by these different methods can be severe.

A variety of grouts have also been developed to fill voids within the ground and so bind weak soil. If a cement or chemically based

Figure 7 Confined operation of machinery resulting in repeated trafficking and therefore disturbance of underlying deposits (Photo: Mike Brice)

grout is used inappropriately archaeological remains may be both physically encased and chemically altered by the grout. The chemistry of grouts is discussed further by Karol (1990). Examples of grouting operations are shown on Figures 8, 9 and 10.

Depending on the character of archaeological remains and the burial environment in which they are preserved, any alteration of a site's groundwater regime during ground improvement may create a significant construction impact. For example, groundwater-abstraction methods are most likely to have an impact on archaeological remains that are preserved within a waterlogged and anaerobic burial environment. The impacts can include the ingress of oxygen and other oxidising chemical species into a waterlogged deposit, for example by the lowering of a water table allowing an introduction of air into the burial environment, or from transport of dissolved chemicals as a result of changed groundwater flows. The threat to the continuing preservation of *in situ* archaeological remains at a site affected by dewatering is acknowledged and increasing interest is being paid to the options for groundwater modelling as a means to design groundwater amelioration systems (Welch and Thomas 1998).

2.3.3 Mitigation of impact from engineering operations used during pre-construction activities

Before commencement of the pre-construction activities, the archaeological sensitivity of a development site should largely be known. Therefore, provided good communication exists between the engineer and archaeologist, it should be possible to mitigate construction impact by careful zoning of the site. Zoning involves reaching agreement on the types of engineering operations permitted in each part of the site in order that construction impact is avoided in areas of archaeological sensitivity.

However, the adoption of zoning (ie avoidance) as a total archaeological mitigation strategy may not be possible on many sites. This might be due to the high density or sensitivity of archaeological remains present, or to the specific development requirements needed to construct the new building. In these cases increased effort is needed to use mitigation options that minimise the possible disturbance of ground caused by the pre-construction activities. A summary of the main options to avoid or limit pre-construction impact on archaeological remains is now discussed.

Limited zoning may be possible by careful management of the location and construction of access roads, accommodation and storage areas, vehicle-turning areas, etc. At all times, advice from archaeologists should be sought, such that a workable management and site plan can be achieved during the site-preparation activities.

Consideration could be given to avoiding the need for ground intrusion by locating temporary drains, service lines (eg water and electricity) and temporary ground footings (eg supporting site fencing) above ground. In addition, the option of temporarily reusing existing service ducting and surviving fencing or hoarding and their footings should be explored.

The discovery of unexpected ground conditions or buried obstructions can require a revision to the scheme of working

Figure 8   Construction of a large grouting shaft (Photo: Mike Brice)

Figure 9 Medieval walls within a large grouting shaft at Parliament Square, for the Jubilee Line Extension (Photo: Museum of London Archaeology Service)

Figure 10 Part of a medieval skeleton under excavation by MoLAS. Grouting material escaped into the archaeological deposits, following paths of least resistance, when some grouting tubes such as the one shown here split (Photo: Museum of London Archaeology Service)

agreed between the engineer and archaeologist. The establishment of good communication between the two professions can increase the likelihood of the revisions being agreed without excessive cost over-runs or damage to the archaeological remains. This may require the identification and precise locating of the buried obstructions by way of a staged investigation, possibly using geophysical surveying techniques and small-scale excavation, rather than indiscriminate pile probing and large-scale excavation.

The need for communication and agreement between the engineer and archaeologist is important if ground improvement or *in situ* remediation of contamination is to form part of the construction process, since this involves a variety of engineering operations that can dramatically alter existing 'undisturbed' ground conditions. Of particular concern is that the operations are frequently employed in the near-surface soil horizons in which the archaeological remains are generally located. If the final building solution cannot be redesigned to avoid the need for ground improvement or land-contamination remediation, then an over-riding objective of a mitigation strategy should be to isolate the archaeology from the area to be affected by these activities. For example, isolation of waterlogged remains during dewatering activities can be undertaken by their containment with impermeable membranes and bunds; a recharge trench supplied with pumped water can also be constructed if active maintenance of a high water table is required. Isolation of the archaeology may be achieved by modification of the selected engineering technique, for example injection of grout (during ground improvement) and microbes (for bioremediation of contamination) into inclined boreholes can successfully avoid overlying remains. In addition to confining ground improvement to a controlled area, the technique selected should be of low impact and chemically non-aggressive to the archaeology, for example possible avoidance of both high-pressure jet grouting and sodium silicate grouts (which can form sodium chloride as a by-product in the ground). A mitigation strategy may be necessary to ensure time is allowed for archaeological remains and burial environments to re-equilibrate during the improvement of ground conditions, for example the use of surcharging rather than dynamic compaction to give a slow improvement in soil strength.

Another form of ground improvement is the removal of weak soils by stripping, which in the past has often been regarded as a straightforward civil-engineering operation. The planning conditions applied to development projects and the value now given to soil by engineers (eg for landscaping and off-site sale) has changed this attitude. Although developed for achieving high-quality land restoration and not for minimising disturbance to archaeology, there are a variety of soil-moving protocols which minimise ground disturbance (RMC 1985). These protocols include: the avoidance of earth scrapers in favour of excavators and dump trucks; adaptation of plant to reduce ground compaction (eg low-pressure tyres); and guidelines for the timing of operations (eg use of field tests for soil-moisture determination). Refinement of these protocols as part of a mitigation strategy, and their subsequent supervised implementation, will act to reduce unacceptable construction impact.

In all instances the potential for impact to archaeology on the site will be minimised if there is close consultation between the engineer, archaeological consultant and local planning officer.

2.4 Stage 3: Construction activities

2.4.1 Engineering operations used during construction activities

The operations employed during the main phase of construction activity generally have one of two purposes: those concerned with the construction of structures and buildings, and those connected with earthwork construction. Engineering operations used during both types of construction are described in Appendix A (Section A3.0), and a summary is given below.

Structures and buildings

During this stage of a project, the engineering operations that can potentially create the greatest impact on archaeological remains are those connected with the construction of foundations and services.

Foundations can be defined as that part of a structure which directly transmits load to the ground, and they can be either shallow or deep (Cole 1988; Tomlinson 1995). As a guide, shallow foundations often extend to depths of less than 2m but may be as much as 5m (excluding the special case of deep basements), and deep foundations can be taken as being more than 5m deep. If a basement is to be constructed then all soil to the full depth of the basement will be removed by excavation, and additional foundation elements may then be installed below the basement's base.

Shallow foundations are those which generally transfer loads from a building to the near-surface soil. Under normal soil conditions, shallow foundations (ie strip footings, pads and rafts) will yield greater settlement and lower load-carrying capacity, and cost less than deep (ie piled) foundations. Therefore shallow foundations tend to be used on lower-cost projects, where foundation loads are low in comparison to the allowable bearing capacity of the soil, or where settlement (and differential settlement) criteria are not too onerous. Deep foundations tend to be used on projects where foundation loads are high in relation to the allowable bearing capacity of the surface soil, settlement criteria are stringent, or construction factors such as a high water table make shallow foundations less economic due to the difficulties in making the necessary excavations.

Figure 11 Shallow strip footings at the Kaetsu Centre, New Hall, Cambridge (Photo: Cambridge Archaeological Unit)

The stages involved in the selection of a foundation type and its detailed design are usually as follows:

1 Establish the approximate magnitude and geometry of structural loads including allowance for factors such as earthquakes, scour/erosion, etc if appropriate.
2 Determine the bearing capacity of the ground from the results of the ground investigation.
3 Determine the minimum permissible founding depth on the basis of building geometry (eg basement depth), soil conditions (eg thickness of surface peat layer).
4 Determine depth of water table, and other factors affecting construction (eg archaeology).
5 On the basis of the above select foundation type and depth.
6 If justified, check predicted settlement, compare with the tolerance of the proposed structure and review the selection of foundation type and depth.

By using this methodology, a range of foundation options may be available, with shallow foundations usually being considered first because they tend to be the cheaper option. However, this range of options becomes more restricted as the loads increase, strength/stiffness of the soil reduces or settlement criteria become more onerous. Under these conditions the designer may eventu-

ally be constrained to use deep foundations. Environmental and archaeological considerations may further influence the choice of foundation or perhaps overall building design.

If used, shallow foundations basically comprise strip footings, pads and rafts, each of which may be used in combination or isolation to support a structure. Generally speaking, pads support single columns, strip footings support single walls, and rafts support combinations of walls and columns. A raft foundation may be used where the base soil has a low bearing capacity and/or the loads are so large that more then 50 per cent of the building footprint is covered by conventional strip or pad footings (Bowles 1996). The principal of these foundations is to spread the load imposed by the superstructure on to a sufficient area of competent soil such that failure of the soil does not occur and settlement due to compression of the soil is not excessive. Generally for aesthetic reasons, as well as to avoid weak near-surface soils and near-surface seasonal soil movements, such foundations are formed in excavations, characteristically 1–2m deep. Raft foundations may be used for basements to provide the floor slab. Concrete is almost universally used to form the foundations, usually cast *in situ* and possibly with a reinforced steel mesh, because of its durability and economy.

Deep foundations act to shed superstructure loads into strong deposits at depth below the ground surface. This is

Figure 12 Insertion of mini cast in situ *bored pile (non-displacement pile) (Photo: Hunting Technical Services)*

Figure 13 Insertion of cast in situ *bored pile (non-displacement pile) (Photo: Mike Brice)*

usually achieved by constructing piles that are structural members of concrete, timber and/or steel, used to transmit the surface loads to lower levels in a soil or rock mass (either as friction piles or end-bearing piles). Piles can be either displacement or non-displacement piles (Fleming et al 1994). As the name suggests, displacement piles are installed by driving a solid pile into the ground so displacing the soil radially as it progresses. This can cause considerable ground disturbance, the exact degree being dependent largely upon the cross-sectional area of the pile. A secondary classification into low or high displacement piles may be adopted. With non-displacement piles the soil into which the pile is to be installed is excavated using various boring techniques. The pile is then formed in the resulting cavity, generally with concrete that is cast *in situ*.

Piles vary in size from 150mm to approximately 2m in diameter and may be more than 100m deep, though the strong soils found in the UK result in more modest foundation depths. An economical pile depth in the UK is usually taken as 10–30m, depending on the installation method. Piling operations are often conducted from a piling platform which is constructed at ground level from available materials (eg demolition waste and brick debris).

There may be occasions when a combination of shallow and deep foundations is used as the final building solution, for example raft foundations can be supported by piles on sites with high groundwater (ie to control buoyancy) or where the base soil is susceptible to large settlements.

Examples of three different foundation solutions are shown on Figures 11, 12 and 13.

During foundation construction it is likely that service lines will be marked out. If they are to be installed below ground, the excavation of shallow trenches will be necessary in which to lay the drains, pipes, cables, ducting, etc. Larger-scale excavations may also be required to incorporate access chambers (eg inspection chambers, pumping gear or interceptors), install boilers and to connect the services into pre-existing systems.

Earthworks

Earthworks are most likely to be carried out on highways contracts, on reservoir contracts and, in a minor way, on landscaping contracts for other developments. The term 'earthworks' describes the excavation of soil to form cuttings, usually with side slopes but occasionally within retaining walls, and the placement of compacted soil in layers to form embankments.

Ground preparation for embankments usually commences with topsoil stripping, followed by either the removal of small areas of weak ground or the surcharging of larger areas (to increase its strength and reduce settlement after final construction). Cuttings involve the removal of soil commonly to depths of 5m, occasionally to 20m or more. The large scale of many earthworks contracts encourages the use of heavy earth-moving plant, and compaction of the soil within the working area is to be expected.

When soil slopes are formed at angles steeper than can be sustained in the long term by the soil itself, some kind of retaining structure is required. This is constructed in front of the soil slope in order to prevent its failure and can be one of two principal types: the embedded retaining wall and the gravity retaining wall.

2.4.2 Impact of engineering operations used during construction activities

Foundation and earthwork construction involves the use of large, often specialised plant, which is designed to complete the tasks required of it as quickly and efficiently as possible. Historically the subject of minimising ground disturbance in order to reduce construction impact on archaeological remains was a minor consideration. This has, however, changed with the introduction of stricter planning controls, and the requirement of large projects to carry out environmental-impact assessments in which construction impacts on archaeological features have to be assessed (DoE 1989). However, on a particularly sensitive site it is important to realise that unless ground is totally isolated from all construction activity and traffic, the near-surface soils are likely to suffer some degree of disturbance which may impact on archaeological remains.

Excavation creates the greatest direct construction impact on archaeological remains, and typically occurs with most types of foundation, buried services and earthworks. The excavation is often located within deposits near the surface, and this ground is potentially the most archaeologically sensitive. For example, shallow foundations can require all surface 'made ground' within the area of the foundation element to be removed in order to expose the underlying load-bearing subsoil stratum, such that during construction of a raft foundation the entire footprint of the building may be excavated to a depth of 2m or more. Associated with the excavation is the problem of upholding the surrounding ground and dealing with groundwater. This may involve the insertion of retaining structures (eg sheet piling) and dewatering measures (eg wellpoints).

The construction of foundation elements or earthworks on the ground surface will also create a load that did not previously exist. Such a load can cause compaction of the underlying ground and on some sites a tendency for soils to spread laterally (eg in soft soils under an embankment). The resulting construction impact on *in situ* archaeological remains may therefore be severe. In addition to the overall increase in load,

a rapid application of load during a construction project may give the archaeological deposits insufficient time to react to the change in ground conditions. This can result, for example, in brittle failure rather than plastic deformation of artefacts.

Compared to a raft foundation, excavation for pads and strip footings may not be as destructive; however, they do require excavation of pits and trenches which can divide the remaining unexcavated soil into a number of cells. This reduces the archaeological value of a deposit by limiting the scope for cross-correlation across the site.

Piled foundations may be preferable to pads and strip footings (shallow foundations) insofar as the area of ground disturbance per unit load carried is less for piles. Such an advantage may be lost because rarely does a foundation consist of a single pile. Generally there will be a minimum of two or three piles under a foundation element or footing to allow for misalignments and other inadvertent eccentricities. Unless a single pile is used, a cap is necessary which spreads the vertical and horizontal loads and any overturning movements to all the piles in the group. Pile caps are usually constructed below ground level for aesthetic reasons and therefore require large excavations. Even when a single pile is used the construction impact may be viewed as high because there is total loss of archaeology within the area occupied by the pile (Figure 14), and further disturbance of *in situ* remains in the surrounding ground may occur. Ground heave and the physical disturbance of remains due to distortion caused by the passage of driven piles through them can be severe (Dalwood et al 1994). Other potential impacts from piling on surrounding *in situ* archaeological remains include the bending down of deposits, introducing oxygen into previously oxygen-free deposits and the puncturing of previously sealed deposits causing water to drain away from them (see Section 3.1.2 and Biddle 1994). Similar construction impacts from the piling of waterlogged archaeological sites in London have been reported, which include the deposits being 'liquefied' and an estimation that a 10 per cent destructive pile grid may be 40 per cent destructive at the water table (Nixon 1998).

These impacts and the physical disturbance of deposits due to excessive ground vibration and soil heave are most severe during the driving in of large displacement piles. The impact may be particularly severe if piles are caused to deviate from their vertical line due to buried obstructions. Though estimates of the degree of ground-surface movement (up 0.5m around piles) and volumes of soil affected by heave (up to 60 per cent of the volume of the pile) are available for such piles, they are very much related to specific soil types and site conditions (Fleming et al 1994; Broms 1981). Therefore, caution must be exercised if they are used to assess the impact of a particular pile type on a site containing archaeological deposits.

During the excavations required for foundations the impact from construction may extend to archaeological

Figure 14 MoLAS excavations at 1 Poultry, London. The Roman polychrome mosaic floor was scarcely displaced right up to the edge of the 1960s' piles (Photo: Museum of London Archaeology Service)

remains outside the excavated area. The construction of piles often involves the use of heavy plant which may rut and compact ground surfaces. Piling platforms used to limit such ground disturbance can themselves create a construction impact due to resulting compaction from the combined load of the platform and plant. The import of material to construct the platform may also act aggressively on the *in situ* archaeology. If large volumes of spoil are produced from an excavation or stripped area, its storage on surrounding land may impose unacceptable loads or introduce contaminated material to the archaeologically sensitive ground. Long-term storage of soils may cause physical, chemical and biological changes within the underlying ground. For example, a shift can occur from aerobic to anaerobic conditions as the soil's bulk density increases, porosity and gas exchange decreases and biological activity decreases.

Compounding the potential impact of foundation excavation, the chemical composition of foundation materials may create a construction impact on archaeological remains. For example, concrete is by far the most popular material for the construction of foundations. It is usually a mixture of water, sand, aggregate and cement, where the cement is typically composed of 80 per cent carbonated lime and 20 per cent clay

(eg Portland cement) (Slater 1983). Concrete is a highly alkaline material that can be poured as a wet mixture into direct contact with the ground, for example down boreholes to construct non-displacement piles or in shallow trenches to form strip footings. If the introduction of concrete to a burial environment causes the generation of heat (curing of concrete is an exothermic reaction), a raised pH and an increased cation concentration, the resulting construction impacts may act as agents of decay in certain archaeological remains. For example, an increase in ionic composition of an aqueous solution may initiate corrosion of a buried metal artefact (Edwards 1998).

As briefly mentioned, the introduction of foundations, embedded retaining walls and other below-ground structures can have an impact on a site's hydrogeological regime. This may occur if they act as physical barriers to the movement of water into and out of a site, so resulting in a change in the level and quality of water surrounding *in situ* archaeological remains (Figure 15). There is also evidence of foundations acting as pathways for the movement of salts through a site, for example capillary movement of water within a pile followed by evaporation at the surface can allow salt crystallisation (efflorescence) to occur (English Heritage 1994).

Figure 15 Possible dewatering that has caused shrinkage of wet organic deposits in York (demonstrated by the void between the surface concrete slab and underlying deposits) (Photo: Hunting Technical Services)

2.4.3 Mitigation of impact from engineering operations used during construction activities

By this stage of a project, mitigation strategies designed to avoid, reduce or remove the impact of construction activities should form part of the approved engineering design and contractor's method statement.

Many of the construction activities discussed involve engineering operations that may have also been used during the previous two stages of a development project (ie during a ground investigation and the pre-construction activities). Therefore the mitigation options discussed in Sections 2.4 and 2.5 may also be applicable to this stage of a project. For example, the excavation of ground during the construction of shallow foundations, service lines or earthworks uses similar equipment to that used during a ground investigation. However, if the mitigation strategy being followed for a highly sensitive site that contains extensive and thinly stratified archaeological remains prevents the use of mechanical excavation, then hand digging of shallow and narrow excavations may be necessary. A discussion of this approach to the hand digging of service trenches is given for a site in Bourton on the Water, Gloucestershire (Woodiwiss 1998).

To mitigate against 'accidental damage' to *in situ* archaeological remains both the developer or resident engineer and archaeologist should be fully aware of all aspects of the construction method statement, and any agreed restricted practice procedures must be effectively communicated to individual contractors on a site. Good communication can stress the importance of observing the boundaries of protected areas and ensures any changes to otherwise standard construction procedures are conveyed to the various short-term contractors engaged in specific tasks (eg demolition teams, piling rig crews, service engineers, etc). This can be achieved by regular briefing meetings between the engineer, contractors and archaeologist, and the use of signs across the site. In addition, an archaeological watching brief may be required to supervise all engineering operations which involve some form of ground disturbance, and to verify the successful adoption of agreed mitigation strategies.

Careful planning and the use of suitably experienced contractors during foundation construction (ie those familiar with working on archaeologically sensitive sites) are vital to avoid unnecessary construction impacts. The construction of piled foundations in particular is a skilled operation and problems may arise due to lack of care by the contractor. They may unintentionally cause contamination, rutting or compaction of ground surfaces, and an increased area of below-ground disturbance around the pile as it is constructed. These problems may be compounded by insufficient information on ground conditions and the presence of buried obstructions, leading to incorrect specifications being followed or the wrong type of pile used. Avoidance of this potential problem is achieved by ensuring that this information provided from the ground investigation and pre-construction stage is fully documented and made available during this stage of the project.

The information may require that before piling commences, ground surfaces are protected with membranes and load-spreading mats. Then if obstructions are encountered they should be investigated and removed (if archaeologically acceptable), or bored to enable piling to continue without relocating the pile or causing it to deviate from its intended path during construction (thus disturbing a larger area of deposit).

The avoidance or minimisation of the extent and depth of excavation on archaeologically sensitive ground during all foundation or earthwork constructions should be a key objective in any mitigation strategy. For example, as the insertion of a basement requires excavation of ground to the full depth of the basement, it may be possible to confine this component of a building to archaeologically barren areas. Alternatively, the basement could be reduced in height, or its function designed as an above-ground location (eg permit an additional storey on a building to create a roof-top car park). Disturbance during foundation construction may also be reduced if a building design permits foundations to be located only on previously disturbed ground, such as use of pad footings that respect the foundation geometry of a previously standing building. Alternatively, if ground conditions permit, ground-intrusive elements of the foundation design could be raised above ground level, such as raft foundations, pile caps and ground beams.

If retaining structures are required to support ground surrounding an excavation they should again be selected to cause minimal ground disturbance. For example, a retaining wall formed by sheet piling would create a thin-walled impermeable barrier that may impact on archaeological deposits to a lesser degree than if a king post and plank construction wall was used. If groundwater control is required to construct the retaining wall, it may be possible to avoid the use of dewatering operations and instead temporarily isolate the archaeologically sensitive ground with an impermeable membrane. Alternatively, carefully controlled grouting of the ground in which the retaining structure is to be formed will confine the zone of ground disturbance to a smaller area than may be caused by wellpoint dewatering.

A mitigation strategy to minimise the impact of pile construction on *in situ* archaeological remains must include an analysis of loads imposed by the new development. In this way, and if justified, it may be possible to use a non-standard or novel design for the development that will permit a less ground-intrusive foundation solution to be used on the site. Novel designs as opposed to 'off the peg' designs are perhaps more common on urban development projects because ground conditions are generally more complex, and there is often a planning requirement for conformity to the surrounding built environment. The incorporation of mitigation strategies into the 'off the peg' designs that are more commonly used for projects in rural locations where the development value is often lower can be difficult, largely because of the reluctance of developers to consider more novel and potentially costly building designs. A final observation for both novel and 'off the peg' designs is that potential construction impacts may be minimised by avoiding using overengineered foundation designs. However, this mitigation option may not be possible because of the stringent building regulations to which developers have to comply.

A novel building design may involve revising a building solution to that of a framed structure which avoids the use of piles or at least permits a reduction in the number of piles in the foundation design (McGill 1995). If the use of piles cannot be avoided by a change in design of the final development, mitigation options to limit ground disturbance may involve revising the type, number, spacing, size and depth of pile that is to be used. For example, replacement rather than displacement piles may be adopted as ground vibration and movement can be less severe, drilling tools can break up buried obstructions to reduce pile deviation (not applicable when using continuous flight auger piles), larger-diameter piles can be constructed, and deposit samples can be recovered for inspection during coring. Because the removal of obstructions is often undertaken by machines that cause a large cone of excavation down to the obstruction, mitigation options may include use of bored cast *in situ* piles. Piling rigs that construct these piles can make use of chisels or more appro-

priately a core barrel which will further confine the area of ground disturbance to the cross-sectional area of the pile only. The incorporation of long-span post-tensioned flat concrete slabs and ground beams has been used to increase the piling grid spacing and so reduce the area of site penetrated by the piles. This approach has been applied to sites where the '5 per cent' rule (ie the area of ground disturbance should not exceed 5 per cent of the footprint of the building to be constructed) has been used to evaluate the potential impact of a foundation solution; for example, long-span slabs and larger-diameter piles on a commercial development enabled a $6m^2$ piling grid (ie a foundation pile would penetrate the archaeological deposits every 6m) to be increased to $12m^2$, which reduced the number of pile penetrations by about 60 per cent and the direct physical disturbance to the archaeology to under 2 per cent (Tilly 1998). Though criticism has been made of the 5 per cent rule because it is possible for disturbance of the archaeology to extend beyond the cross-sectional area of each pile, a mitigation strategy that increases the piling grid spacing will reduce the impact of construction on a site of archaeological importance (Figure 16).

Alternatively, the piles or other foundation elements could be relocated to avoid areas of archaeological sensitivity, such as use of cantilevered beams to span the sensitive ground (McGill 1995). An example of the avoidance of archaeological remains by foundation elements is shown on Figure 17. Relocation as a mitigation strategy is perhaps more applicable to rural sites on which there can be a greater flexibility on the location of the footprint of a new building and the associated, and potentially less archaeologically damaging, landscaping and surface car parking. Relocation and the revision of a piling grid layout can include the direct reuse of redundant foundations, or the excavation and boring out of old foundations by a 'Fondedile' piling rig before replacement with new minipiles (Ove Arup 1991; 1997). Provided the geotechnical engineer is satisfied of the soundness of these approaches on a project, they can avoid the need for extensive excavation of undisturbed and thus potentially archaeologically sensitive ground. However, there is often inadequate documentation on the design assumptions made at the time of a previous construction, which often acts as a hindrance to the reuse of existing foundations by engineers.

The reporting and careful archiving of foundation solutions and mitigation strategies adopted for each construction project is therefore an option needed to overcome this problem should a site emerge for future redevelopment.

Careful planning and on-site verification of a foundation design by an archaeologist and engineer are important because this can ensure that minimal disturbance of the *in situ* archaeology is achieved. In addition this may avoid the use of unplanned and potentially damaging operations, such as increasing the piling platform depth to support a larger piling rig or additional plant. This on-site checking may form part of an archaeological watching brief, as would be detailed within a planning permission's Section 106 agreement.

Figure 16 Surrounded by the piled foundations of the Queen's Building at Emmanuel College, Cambridge, the remains of the 13th-century Black Friars priory were preserved beneath imported material and a geotextile membrane (Photo: Cambridge Archaeological Unit)

Figure 17   Ground beams located over medieval settlement remains at Corpus Christi College's Benet Court redevelopment, Cambridge. Although this site was subsequently excavated, the judicious location of ground beams to avoid archaeological remains can be used in avoidance mitigation strategies (Photo: Cambridge Archaeological Unit)

In addition to mitigating the impact of excavation associated with the construction of foundations, it may be necessary to mitigate against the impact of introducing new materials into the ground. During foundation construction, this is most likely to occur when concrete is used. On sensitive sites one or more of the following mitigation options may be necessary:

1 Insertion of an impermeable membrane between the archaeology and concrete, eg line shallow trenches with membrane before pouring of concrete to form strip footings, and sleeving of cast-in-place concrete piles with either flexible or rigid uPVC.
2 Replacement of concrete with a less aggressive material in areas of archaeological sensitivity, eg use of stone or brick for shallow foundations, and timber or preformed steel piles instead of concrete piles.
3 Use pre-cast concrete rather than cast *in situ*, eg pre-cast raft foundations and preformed piles.
4 Limit the depth of excavation to leave a buffering zone of *in situ* soil between the archaeology and concrete, or use a controlled backfill material to form a buffer (eg sand).

The avoidance of casting concrete *in situ* is not always practical; however, attention could be paid to the quantity of water used in mixing concrete as relatively very little water is needed to actually set concrete, but more is used to ensure the concrete remains at a workable consistency when pouring (Neville and Brooks 1997). If acceptable to the engineer, a reduction in water used could lessen the potential impact of contaminated water draining down into the archaeological deposits.

2.5 Stage 4: Post-construction remedial and maintenance activities

2.5.1 Engineering operations used during remedial and maintenance activities

In addition to producing new developments, the construction industry is responsible for maintaining, improving and adapting the existing stock of buildings, roads, etc. Therefore, after completion of a development, it may be necessary to carry out the following operations which could have an impact on archaeological remains:

1 Buildings:
    i) underpinning of shallow foundations
    ii) repair of ground-bearing slabs
2 Services (cleaning, repair, renovation and renewing):
    i) water supply
    ii) drainage
    iii) gas

    iv) telecommunications
    v) electricity
3 Roads and earthworks:
    i) slope failure repairs
    ii) reconstruction
4 Landscaping

These activities are described fully in Appendix A (Section A4.0), and summarised below.

Buildings

Underpinning may be accomplished by the formation of a strip footing below the existing wall, or by piling beneath the existing wall. The strip-footing method involves substantial excavations below the wall, while piles, generally of small diameter, may be less disruptive (Hunt et al 1991). Ground-bearing slabs are usually laid on a bed of hard-core (granular material) and, unless a cracked slab is to be totally reformed or the hard-core replaced, the underlying strata will not be disturbed during its repair. Replacement of the hard-core, which would involve excavation and possible ground disturbance, may occur if it was found to be the cause of the slabs' failure (eg sulphate attack).

Services

Underground services have traditionally been maintained or replaced by trench excavation; the impact caused by trenching is illustrated in Figure 18. More recently, however, to reduce the disruption to surface activities which trenching causes, trenchless or minimum dig technologies have been adopted, particularly by the gas and water industries. Though limited excavation is still required, the adoption of this approach should reduce the potential for impact to archaeological remains.

Roads and earthworks

On roads and earthworks a variety of techniques have been developed to repair slope failures (slips). Traditionally the entire slipped mass was removed and replaced with granular material. Alternatively, the slipped soil can be strengthened (eg using geotextiles, grouting or soil-nailing methods) or restrained (eg with gabions) before being reused. All these approaches involve heavy equipment which are generally used for the movement, removal and importation of soils and materials.

Road surfaces may need repairing, the operations for which can range from simply rejuvenating the wearing surface with a coat of bitumen and chippings, to a total replacement of the road construction. In the majority of cases, the 'formation', which is the original excavation level upon which the road was constructed, will not be disturbed during maintenance. If total replacement of the road construction occurs, for example in road realignment or widening to provide additional carriageway, this should be viewed

Figure 18 A late 2nd-century building beneath Borough High Street during MoLAS excavations for London Underground Limited Jubilee Line Extension; areas of truncation from Victorian sewers are clearly visible (Photo: Museum of London Archaeology Service)

Figure 19 Remedial measure to improve the drainage of a landscaped area by the insertion of a slit drain, creating a potential physical impact on in situ *archaeology (Photo: Hunting Technical Services)*

as new construction rather than maintenance. Maintenance may, however, involve the excavation for, and then replacement or installation of, drains on one or both sides of the carriageway.

Landscaping

Failure of a landscaping scheme may necessitate the use of a variety of engineering operations which can include removal and importation of topsoil, replacement of dead vegetation, repair and installation of drains and intensive use of agrochemicals (Figure 19).

2.5.2 Impact of engineering operations used during remedial and maintenance activities

As a general rule remedial and maintenance activities do not require planning permission. Therefore, unless the archaeology has been given statutory protection, it is possible for these activities to be carried out without any archaeological involvement. Fortunately, the majority of remedial and maintenance activities are carried out above ground and so will have little or no impact on buried archaeological remains, for example road resurfacing and most vegetation control. In addition, excavations during the repair of below-ground services generally involve ground that has previously been disturbed during construction of the original development.

However, potential construction impacts on archaeological remains can still occur if the maintenance activities involve new excavations, for example underpinning, repair of ground-bearing slabs and roads, or installation of new drains and other services. The removal by excavation and/or importation of new material may impact on archaeology if ground heave or compaction occurs due to changes in the ground-bearing load. Finally, poorly located and badly conducted excavations may extend the zone of ground disturbance into archaeologically sensitive areas.

Landscaping and vegetation control may create an unacceptable impact if agrochemicals are used which then leach into the underlying archaeological deposits. Ground disturbance and impact on near-surface archaeological remains may occur through the inappropriate timing and use of machinery. For example, a combination of wet ground conditions and overpowered machines (eg farm machinery used on a landscaping scheme) is likely to lead to unwanted ground disturbance. The number, location and species selection of new trees and shrubs should be considered because of the physical disturbance their rooting systems could have on the buried archaeological resource.

2.5.3 Mitigation of impact from engineering operations used during remedial and maintenance activities

In the same manner as the previous three stages of a construction project, the *in situ* archaeological remains of a site must be considered when designing a programme of maintenance. This applies to specific repair or remediation operations (eg underpinning), and maintenance activities conducted on a regular basis (eg drain cleaning).

Maintenance activities that cause ground disturbance will generally involve engineering operations that are also used during the construction of a new development, therefore mitigation options will usually employ principles already discussed in this report.

If justified, a mitigation strategy may include the use of specialist repair and maintenance contractors who operate equipment designed to specifically minimise ground disturbance. Though generally not developed for application on archaeological sites, options available include the trenchless rehabilitation of sewers, in which a variety of liners, closed-circuit television and robotic repairs are used (Read 1997). Particularly sensitive ground conditions may also require the use of modified groundworks equipment, for example specialist ground maintenance on golf courses to avoid rutting, compaction and the disturbance of near-surface irrigation lines (DoE 1992).

It is important, however, to ensure that when maintenance activities do occur they are first brought to the attention of an archaeologist. The assessment by an archaeologist will ensure that the activities do not have a direct impact on the archaeology, and do not affect the integrity of an engineered mitigation strategy which may already be installed at the site.

3.0 LITERATURE REVIEW AND RESEARCH PRIORITIES

3.1 Literature review

A comprehensive review of published and unpublished literature has been prepared in terms of its relevance to the issue of understanding and mitigating the impact of construction on archaeological remains (Appendix D). It includes an annotated bibliography of both UK and overseas references obtained from a variety of sources, including the British Library, University of Cambridge Library and departmental libraries, English Heritage, individual private organisations, Local Authorities and the Internet.

3.1.1 Review of existing knowledge

Despite extensive literature on the practical use of different ground-engineering techniques that are regularly deployed on sites containing archaeological remains, it appears that engineering solutions are rarely applied to archaeological mitigation problems. Moreover, there is very little 'hard fact' regarding the effects of different engineering techniques on the archaeological record, nor very much published reference data on which processes occur under different environmental conditions. It would appear that engineering solutions are rarely utilised to their full extent in relation to the mitigation of construction impact on archaeological remains.

The published literature that does exist is dominated by North American references, indicating that American archaeologists have been concerned (in print) with issues of *in situ* preservation for a longer period than has been the case in the UK. Nevertheless, data collected for this study show that British archaeological organisations have been developing strategies to mitigate construction impacts on archaeology for about two decades. Many of the examples concern urban environments where deep, complex stratigraphy prevails, particularly on sites within London and York. However, such mitigation strategies are seldom published unless they serve to illustrate the methodological effectiveness or otherwise of the strategy.

Compared to England, the US experimental projects appear to show a more concerted effort at predictive modelling, significance testing to assist in strategic planning, experimentation in preservation methods and the impacts of construction

on archaeology generally. With an emphasis on preservation *in situ* now firmly ingrained in British archaeological planning, archaeologists and developers are beginning to question the reliability of preservation methods as well as the physical-biological-chemical effects of all manner of construction processes. The North American references (in Appendix D) should therefore provide an important data set that can assist in devising schemes to test the effects of construction impacts and, in some cases, the development of mitigation strategies themselves.

The principal engineering and planning response with respect to archaeology is to use avoidance schemes (a discussion of the database results in the supplementary report demonstrates this). However, where engineered solutions are required, various forms of piling and rafting are commonly utilised in urban areas, while rafting and embanking are often used in rural areas, especially on new road schemes and industrial complexes. Nonetheless, the archaeological and planning professions have very little knowledge of the direct consequences on the archaeological record of the most commonly used types of engineering techniques. For example, what are the real effects of continuous piling on the physical-chemical state of the archaeological sediments and materials such as upstanding structures, feature fills, inorganic and organic remains, the preservation status of these materials, the ambient water table and the radius of effect of the piling on the total archaeological record? Under rafting or embankment schemes, we have only sketchy knowledge of the changes through time on the physical-chemical-biological environment of burial, for example changes in oxygen and pH status in the soil, interruption of groundwater and soil-moisture flows, and compression. In summary, the burial environment and the processes associated with it (natural processes and construction-influenced processes) are poorly understood. In addition, much of the research that has been published is by researchers from disciplines other than archaeology, that is, agricultural and engineering.

3.1.2 Experimental and monitoring projects

There are several current experimental research and monitoring projects which are providing some insights into the nature of the preservation environment associated with archaeological deposits under prescribed environmental conditions, for example the two experimental earthwork sites at Wareham on acidic sands and at Overton Down on calcareous chalk downland (Jewell 1963; Hillson 1996; Bell et al 1996), and the Soil Archive Classification programme (Wagner et al 1997). Soil-moisture and groundwater monitoring schemes in urban and rural situations are also in progress at several archaeological sites throughout England, namely the Rose Theatre (Davis 1994), York (Davis 1996), Market Deeping (Corfield 1996) and Willingham/Over (French and Davis 1994), as well as a completed study of anaerobic burial environments (Caple and Dungmore 1996). The wider use of remote data collection methods (use of geophysical surveying techniques, permanently installed and logged probes and sensors) is gradually beginning, but the range of sites being monitored and the number of available monitoring devices could be usefully expanded. This requirement for monitoring archaeological sites has been recognised to some degree by the Natural Environment Research Council (NERC) in its Urban Regeneration and the Environment programme or 'URGENT'. The Royal Commission on Environmental Pollution also noted in its report on devising a soil-protection policy that attention should be paid to the requirements of archaeological conservation (Royal Commission 1996). Ideally this will be achieved through a programme of research, possibly within the subject area of geoarchaeological investigation.

Several conservation schemes which have involved the preservation of archaeological remains *in situ* in wetland environments have been developed, although there has rarely been one directly associated with development and construction (Coles 1995). The factors responsible for the survival and degradation of specific types of environmental evidence are also under investigation, such as Briggs' and Evershed's study of beetle remains (1996) and Collinson et al's (1996) research into the environmental requirements responsible for the preservation of plant cuticles. Occasionally evaluation studies of environmental remains have provided insights into mechanisms responsible for the recent decay of organic remains, such as in medieval York (Carrott et al 1996). There are also several useful studies relating the mechanisms of subsidence (Carbognin and Gatto 1986) and the charge and recharge of groundwater (Freeze and Banner 1970). Finally, there are a very few relevant experimental projects which have examined how best to protect archaeological sites from construction damage (ie Ardito 1994, see below), and from excavation sites where the effects of piling have been observed and measured such as Farrier Street in Worcester (Dalwood et al 1994).

Overton Down and Wareham experimental earthworks are the most comprehensively studied experimental archaeological sites in the UK. These experimental earthworks were set up in 1960 in order to test the preservation of organic and inorganic materials and assess processes of weathering over time (Bell et al 1996). Among some of the more important transformations,

the old land surface and lowest turf of the rampart were shown to have compressed by a factor of two to three times over two years beneath the weight of the earthwork, followed by stabilisation at Wareham (ibid, 215, 233); whereas compression of the turf stack occurred over four years at Overton (ibid, 233). The variable destruction of different organic materials over the relatively short period of burial is, perhaps, one of the most well-known results from the two experimental projects, but more especially at Overton Down. Obviously, the direct construction impact is limited only to the erection of a bank and a ditch cut into chalk, and therefore is not as potentially destructive as modern construction techniques. Unfortunately there has been no dedicated monitoring of changes in groundwater and soil-moisture content under the banks themselves.

The soil-moisture and groundwater monitoring programmes which are currently underway at Market Deeping, Lincolnshire, and Willingham/Over, Cambridgeshire, have been in operation since the early and mid 1990s, respectively (French et al 1999). Both are on gravel-terrace subsoils where lowland river-terrace valleys meet the fen edge, and the monitoring results have revealed both expected and unexpected results. For example, it was expected that irrigation by the farmers and seasonal variation in rainfall would have a short-term effect on the topsoil-moisture levels, but that this would be effectively negated by crop-moisture take-up, and rarely would affect the buried archaeological levels.

At Market Deeping there appears to be very little change in the soil-moisture content below 400mm which reflects the natural recharge and more impermeable nature of the sandy clay on gravel subsoil. By comparison at Willingham/Over, there is much more fluctuation of the soil-moisture levels and groundwater table due to the more porous sands and gravels of the subsoil below, and the relatively impermeable alluvial silty clays above. On the other hand, the dramatic and changing differences in terms of soil moisture and dissolved oxygen content at different depths in the Willingham profiles suggest that the preservation potential at different levels of burial and in different soil matrices varies considerably and almost independently depending on depth and soil structure. Only rarely are completely anaerobic conditions attained, yet there is reasonable pollen preservation in the buried soil and earthfast features (Wiltshire 1997). In many cases, it is postulated that organic preservation is as much dependent on the absence of disturbance and soil textural and composition factors as on the proximity to the water table and the absolute degree of waterlogging. There now lies the challenge of applying this knowledge to urban sites where the hydrological regime affecting the archaeological deposits is generally many times more complex.

An evaluation study of archaeological and organic remains carried out at 44–45 Parliament Street in York of medieval deposits (Carrott et al 1996) has demonstrated the detrimental effects of recent building techniques on the preservation of the organic record. Dewatering associated with the construction of a recently demolished building combined with the down-movement of salts derived from an overlying concrete slab has caused recent deterioration in the preservation status of plants, parasites and insect remains. This is the first time that such a dramatic and recent deterioration in organic remains has been observed in 20 years of intensive archaeological work in York's city centre. The extensive use of concrete rafts and slabs, as well as crushed limestone for backfilling and under-floor hard-core could pose a very serious problem to continuing organic preservation in urban areas such as York. Without further and immediate testing, much of medieval York that is believed to be reasonably well preserved beneath basement and cellar level could in fact be a fast-diminishing resource.

During excavation fieldwork conducted in advance of construction at Farrier Street in Worcester, the documented effect of driven piles on the late Roman deposits demonstrated the distortion of archaeological deposits occurring for up to 300mm to either side of the pile and over a vertical height of up to 300mm (Dalwood et al 1994). If the diameter of the piles is also taken into account, a minimum area of approximately 700mm in diameter has been distorted. The excavator in this case estimated that 3 per cent of the 2300m² building imprint was affected in this way. Obviously if the pile spacing was closer, the zones of distortion would be much increased. Moreover, the extent of disturbance by the piles was greater than had been expected before construction began (Figures 20, 21).

Similar evidence of distortion caused by piling operations was seen during the re-excavation of newly inserted piles on a waterlogged site at Bergen in Norway, where both stratigraphic

distortion and organic decay occurred as a direct result of the construction technique (Biddle 1994, 8–10). The problem is that there is rarely a chance to observe this effect on archaeological deposits after the construction phase is completed, yet it is becoming critical that such observations are formally conducted in order to understand the effects of foundation construction on a variety of archaeological contexts (wet/dry, waterlogged/solid structures, etc).

Very few experiments have been carried out on archaeological sites on methods of reducing the effects of the impact of construction techniques on the archaeological record. One notable exception is the short-term (3–4 months) experiment carried out on two prehistoric native Indian flint-scatter sites in association with the construction of a gas pipeline in Canada and the United States, in order to allow heavy equipment to operate within the area of the archaeological sites (Ardito 1994). Both sites were protected with a basal geosynthetic woven-textile filter fabric and a crushed stone fill, c 600mm thick, above. Before and after installation, tests were carried out on the 'buried' soil for pH, particle size, moisture content, compaction and sheer strength, and cultural material recovered before and after burial was compared. Perhaps unexpectedly, no significant changes were observed in terms of any of the measured parameters, but this research project has shown that the effects of heavy earth-moving machinery can be successfully dissipated. It is suggested that this very short-term and small-scale experiment should not lull us into a false sense of security, nor negate the value of future research in this area on a wider and more vulnerable variety of deposits/archaeological site components.

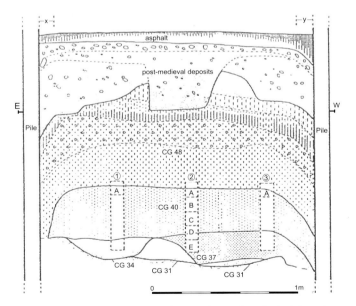

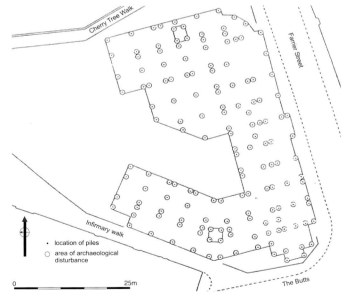

Figure 20 Effects of driven piling on dry archaeological deposits, as demonstrated by a section at Farrier Street, Worcester (Source: Archaeological Services, Worcestershire County Council, Worcestershire Archaeological Society)

Figure 21 Farrier Street, Worcester, showing the location of the piles for the new building and the area of archaeological disturbance around each pile (Source: Archaeological Services, Worcestershire County Council, Worcestershire Archaeological Society)

3.2 Research priorities

The site-specific character of archaeology means that it does not readily lend itself to research of an abstract kind. Also, unless an appropriate research agenda exists that enables the study of impacts, at the moment it is only in unusual circumstances that it is possible to revisit a site to observe what the impact of construction on below-ground archaeology has been because building and engineering projects are generally designed for long lifespans. But, looked at in the broader sense, research has a major role to play as a mechanism for summarising and disseminating the information gathered from the experience of individual projects.

There are two main routes by which knowledge acquired from project experience can be made known to those involved in the design of the construction works:

1   Through archaeological publications and conferences. Generally speaking, those involved with construction do not expect to keep abreast of archaeological scholarship, so information from these sources will only reach them second-hand (usually in discussions with archaeologists on particular projects).

2   Through advice produced by government and other bodies such as the Building Research Establishment, CIRIA (Construction Industry Research and Information Association), the Concrete Society and the Transport Research Laboratory. It is broadly true to say that the advice from such bodies has yet to take account of the implication of PPG 16 for construction projects. At the very least they should refer to PPG 16 and what it means in the type of work in question: in some instances a fuller summary of the archaeological implications of different techniques should be provided.

The majority of construction schemes that affect archaeological remains on a large scale are building developments and new road construction. The former are associated with some form of either raft or pile construction in both urban and rural landscapes, and the latter are often associated with cutting and embanking operations across large swathes of green and/or urban landscapes. To tackle these two major types of building works, the development of new testing and monitoring programmes is essential, carried out as experiments in the laboratory and in the field before, during and after construction. It is inevitable that there will be design, implementation and monitoring costs for years to come with these experiments, and these must be written into the overall development costs from the initial design and planning stage onwards. Moreover, it is crucial in many cases that the monitoring programmes become an integral and required part of the archaeological design brief.

The need for published accounts of research into construction impacts applies across a wide range of construction activities and projects, but there are four areas where new techniques (or the better understanding of existing techniques) require particular attention.

1 Piling

Advice on piling methods should take account of the impact of piling on archaeological remains, emphasising, with examples from completed projects, how the design of piling can be tailored to different types of archaeological deposits. Information concerning the impact of piling (including impacts on adjacent archaeological deposits) will be enlarged by the examination of piles from demolished buildings.

2 Imposed loads

These include the short-term loads from construction traffic and equipment, and the permanent loads from new buildings and structures. The effectiveness of techniques to mitigate the impact of temporary loads, for instance through the use of a piling mat, can be appraised during the course of a project, producing useful feedback for future projects.

3 Grouting

The use of various grouting techniques to control ground movements during construction is gaining in popularity. They all involve consolidation of the ground, and carry the risk that the injected grout may spread further than anticipated. As with other construction techniques, there are unlikely to be opportunities for the retrospective appraisal of the impact of grouting. Since the lateral effects of this consolidation technique are not well understood, this aspect is well suited to significant investigation through simulation studies, or even on a site expressly purchased for impact-testing activities.

4 Building materials

Building materials may have impacts through the leaching of salts into the ground. Laboratory-based tests, covering the main building materials, and the most common substrates and archaeological deposits, could investigate the impact of a variety of building materials.

Ultimately the construction industry should make its members aware of the archaeological implications of building and engineering works. This is best done, not through separate publications dealing with archaeology, but by making archaeological considerations a customary part of advice in all the relevant subject areas.

The highest priority should be to assemble all the available data from engineering literature on various aspects, for instance compaction rates by depth and area of ground affected for as many soil and subsoil types as possible, and groundwater flow and changes in the soil/subsoil chemical environment (Hunter and Currie 1956; Abdul-Kareem and McRae 1984; Ward and Robinson 1990). On the basis of this work, it would then be possible to target the areas of poor or non-existent knowledge, and to devise appropriate experimental monitoring stations, both in the laboratory and in the field. As an example, such experimentation into imposed loads could be conducted along a road-embankment scheme as follows.

A variety of experiments to simulate conditions of burial would be arranged so that the tests could be conducted on at least three major types of substrate, such as gravel, boulder clay and chalk. Compression testing would be undertaken, plus the determination of particle size, bulk density, soil-structural changes, plastic/liquid limits and sheer strength. Repeat tests could initially be conducted under controlled laboratory conditions to produce statistically viable results, and field tests undertaken at development sites. Such sites would need to be identified in advance of construction in order to produce an experimental design for field testing in conjunction with the planning authorities and development engineers. Obviously, the role and insistence of archaeological development control officers would be essential if this approach were to be successful.

Soil properties such as soil-moisture content, groundwater table and flow characteristics, pH status, dissolved oxygen, redox potential, bulk density, soil structure and the degree of compaction with respect to depth of burial could be monitored, improving our current poor understanding of the burial environment and the processes associated with it. Soil store bunds in mineral-extraction quarries, road embankments and rafted structures could provide three contrasting development settings able to provide the range of information essential to the future development of appropriate mitigation strategies where an imposed load poses a serious threat to the continued preservation of significant archaeological remains.

4.0 SUMMARY OF MITIGATION STRATEGIES

4.1 Introduction

The roles that both an archaeologist and engineer may have during all stages of a development project have been described in Section 1.0 of this report. The earliest possible involvement of archaeologists in a project and then their continuing presence during its construction phase have been stressed in order that archaeological mitigation strategies can be designed and then implemented in an acceptable and cost-effective manner. This requires detailed archaeological advice to be sought in advance of the planning application (ie pre-application discussions) and, more importantly, before ground-intrusive operations are permitted on the site (ie intrusive archaeological evaluations and geotechnical ground investigations). Assuming that a site is shown to contain archaeological remains that are to be preserved *in situ*, further archaeological advice may include discussions with the engineer on which engineering operations will be required to complete the new development. Ideally these discussions will result in development proposals being submitted by a promoter or developer that, when implemented, will have negligible impact on the *in situ* archaeological remains present. This process of discussion and agreement between the engineer and archaeologist can be considered to be an 'avoidance mitigation strategy', which is described in more detail in Section 4.2.

The wide range of engineering operations which can be used during a development project and which may result in ground disturbance, and hence a construction impact on surviving buried *in situ* archaeological remains, is described in Section 2.0 and Appendix A of this report. Mitigation options to remove the construction impact or at least limit the potential for these operations causing ground disturbance have also been described. An understanding of the various mitigation options by both the archaeologist and engineer is considered important because, if the total avoidance of ground-intrusive engineering operations is not possible, these options will form a vital part of a project's 'engineered mitigation strategy'. The use of an engineered mitigation strategy and a summary of the mitigation options which may be incorporated within it are described in Section 4.3.

Whether an avoidance or engineered mitigation strategy is adopted, consideration should also be given to including a monitoring component to assess the effectiveness of the adopted site mitigation strategy. This important consideration is discussed in Section 4.4.

4.2 Avoidance mitigation strategies

Following early discussion between the engineers and archaeologists, a development proposal may be adopted in which all archaeologically damaging engineering operations are excluded from an area of archaeological sensitivity, that is, avoidance of ground disturbance and therefore removal of the threat of construction impact on *in situ* remains.

A total avoidance strategy is most often achieved by zoning a site to create areas in which no, or restricted, construction activity is permitted. Each designated area will contain the archaeological remains and most probably a surrounding buffering zone. The size of buffer zone depends on, among other factors, the fragility of the remains, the character of the burial environment and the type of construction impact affecting them.

The area of restricted access should be clearly delineated on the site by fences and appropriate signs, and it should be shown on all design plans of the project. Good project coordination and communication will ensure that the importance of observing such restrictions will be conveyed to all specialist and individual contractors on the site.

A recent example of the successful use of avoidance occurred during the Bull Wharf development project (Ayre 1997). Archaeological evidence had shown that areas of the site represented a nationally important foreshore within which were a well-preserved complex sequence of wharves dating from a late 2nd-century Roman quay through to various medieval wharves. This example is important because it demonstrates that, by seeking the opinions and concerns of all parties involved, a negotiated redesigned building that neither compromised the archaeological remains nor the viability of the development could be achieved. In this case, a mitigation strategy of avoidance was proposed for

Figure 22 Avoidance of an enclosed Iron Age settlement at the ARC Needingworth Quarry, Cambridgeshire (Photo: Cambridge Archaeological Unit)

the preservation *in situ* of a strip of archaeology along approximately one-fifth of the development site. The remaining area of archaeology was preserved by record (excavation). Development of the site can be summarised as: building design; archaeological investigation; discussions of mitigation options; redesign to achieve avoidance; and finally build.

On a large site, avoidance mitigation strategy may be viewed as the most cost-effective mitigation strategy; for example, the design of mineral-extraction sites may permit avoidance (ie sterilisation) of an area of mineral in order to achieve preservation *in situ* of archaeological remains (Figure 22). However, avoidance as a mitigation strategy has two disadvantages: for the developer it is financially undesirable to exclude areas of the site from the development proposals, and secondly, it may not be possible to exclude effectively all construction impacts from the *in situ* archaeological deposits. This second point particularly applies when a complex or fragile burial environment surrounds the archaeological remains. For example, saturated deposits in which organic remains are preserved within an anaerobic environment are very sensitive to remote changes in the water regime of the site, as would be caused by dewatering operations used during ground improvement. On such a site, an avoidance strategy would not be sufficient to remove the construction impact of dewatering, consequently an engineered mitigation strategy may also be needed as part of the overall management plan for the site.

4.3 Engineered mitigation strategies

4.3.1 Introduction

Engineered mitigation strategies generally incorporate active measures which reduce the impact of engineering operations on the ground containing the archaeological remains. A summary

of the main mitigation options is given in Section 4.3.2. Alternatively, engineered mitigation strategies may adopt measures to isolate the *in situ* archaeology from ground disturbance and hence the impact of construction (ie using either a containment system or a covering regime).

Examples of both the containment and covering approach are discussed below, with further site-specific examples being provided by reference to the database which has been compiled as part of this study. Details of the database and the information it contains are provided in Volume 2 of this study, though an example of a specific site in York is included for reference purposes in Appendix C. In this example, planning permission for a proposed housing scheme was granted only after development of a comprehensive and fully integrated mitigation strategy. The agreed strategy was published in a stand-alone document and includes elements of avoidance, foundation redesign, restricted landscaping and preservation by record.

4.3.2 Mitigation options for individual engineering operations

Whichever overall mitigation strategy is adopted on a site a range of specific measures to reduce or avoid the construction impacts from individual engineering operations should be incorporated into it. These measures (mitigation options) have been discussed above and are summarised in Table 1.

4.3.3 Containment systems

A containment system involves the installation of a bund, membrane or similar barrier around the undisturbed ground containing the archaeological remains. On appropriate sites the archaeological remains and their surrounding burial environment are preserved within the enclosed ground despite disruption of the surrounding ground during site development. Although engineering methods to seal the sides and ground surface are relatively commonplace, the insertion of a barrier below the archaeological deposit can be problematic. Such a barrier may be necessary if the ground has to be completely isolated from construction activities which involve, for example, dewatering and grouting.

Geotextiles may be used as barriers to protect ground surfaces during a development, and they can therefore act to isolate archaeological remains from both direct and indirect construction impacts occurring at ground level (eg surface rutting by vehicle movements, and compaction from high point loads). Suitable geotextiles are synthetic fabrics, designed to be durable and last a reasonable length of time in an often hostile soil environment. They are usually made from polyester, nylon, polyethylene and polypropylene, and the fabrics can be woven or knitted into sheets to be used as either large single sheets (membranes) or as strips that are

Mitigation option	Purpose
Round-table meetings and good communication between all professional groups involved in the project	Involvement of archaeologist, engineer and contractor in the mitigation strategy. Improved quality control in project
Documentation with scale drawings and site plans	Detailed methodology for mitigation strategy and standardisation of terminology where possible
Comprehensive desk-top study, followed by a staged ground investigation, possibly using non-invasive techniques	Improves the assessment of the site's archaeological sensitivity, before extensive ground-intrusive investigations are undertaken
Evaluation of all options that are available for construction to achieve a design of 'least impact'	Economic selection of engineering operations that will create the least construction impact on archaeology, possible use of novel designs, eg Styrofoam raft
Modification of standard foundation designs (eg pile type, diameter, depth, spacing, or depth of shallow foundation)	Limit disturbance of archaeologically sensitive areas, eg avoid close spacing of pile clusters and use single but larger-diameter piles on a wider-spaced grid
Supervision of engineering operations by professional archaeologist	Archaeological watching brief during excavations to avoid accidental loss of archaeological remains
Locate ground-intrusive operations on previously disturbed areas or those demonstrably archaeologically barren	Disturbance limitation, eg reuse of existing foundations and services trenches
Route services, footings and foundations above ground	Avoids and reduces ground disturbance
Creation of a buffer zone above ground by importation of material	Avoids surface rutting, high point loads and contamination, eg geogrid or construction of a piling mat above undisturbed ground
Containment or disposal facilities for unwanted water and arising/spoil	Avoids contamination of ground, eg if groundwater encountered during borehole drilling
Use of impermeable membranes	Isolation of archaeology from construction impacts, eg dewatering and liquid contamination
Evaluation of different backfill and construction materials before their use	Avoids introducing materials that may be aggressive to the archaeology, eg soil to backfill excavations and concrete to form foundations
Allowance for unsuitable weather or ground conditions	Avoids rutting of ground by careful timing of machine movements to avoid wet conditions
Use of load-spreading devices on equipment and ground surfaces	Avoids rutting and compaction of ground from engineering operations, eg geogrid laid below road
Use of trained operators in well-maintained equipment that is suitable for the task specified	Limits excessive ground disturbance and avoids accidental overdig of trial pits, ground contamination with oil, etc
Use of specialised equipment/contractors that cause minimal ground disturbance	Not necessarily developed for archaeological sites but examples include 'no-dig' repairs of buried services
Adaptation of equipment to allow for the protection of ground conditions and potential archaeological remains	Avoidance or reduction of ground disturbance, eg low-pressure tyres and load-spreading plates on excavator

Table 1 Mitigation of impact from engineering operations

formed into geogrids. If made impermeable they are termed geomembranes. Vertical barriers include geomembranes which can line service trenches and other excavations, thereby isolating *in situ* archaeology in the surrounding ground from introduced backfill materials (eg pouring of concrete into trenches to form strip footings). Geotextiles are a relatively recent material for use in development projects; however, the range available and their proven track record are increasing rapidly (eg high tear and gas-resistant landfill liners, and containment systems in contaminated land remediation) (Koerner 1990).

A system of membranes (geotextiles and polythene) and an earth bund has been used as part of an engineered mitigation strategy for the preservation *in situ* of a Late Bronze Age waterlogged wooden platform at Flag Fen, Peterborough (Pryor 1992). Using a combination of a containment and covering strategy, a lake was firstly created over approximately two-thirds of the wooden platform and then a visitor centre was erected on the lake. In order that construction of the visitor centre would not impact on the underlying *in situ* archaeological remains, the mitigation strategy also incorporated a Styrofoam raft to create a low-pressure foundation solution. A section through the lightweight 'semi-floating' foundations of the visitor centre is shown in Figure 23.

Membrane barriers may also need to perform a lagging function to avoid the risk of changes in temperature occurring within the *in situ* deposits. This can result from the

curing of cast *in situ* concrete, inappropriate location of boilers and a change in the site's exposure or containment from atmospheric weather conditions.

4.3.4 Covering systems

The isolation of undisturbed ground by a containment system may remove it from the natural soil processes which are responsible for its specific burial environment (eg the input of water to maintain saturated conditions). Therefore, an alternative approach is required to isolate the archaeological remains from the construction activities and to contain them within or below an engineered covering regime. The aim of this approach is to actively maintain the burial environment conditions thought to be responsible for the *in situ* preservation of the remains, while still permitting development at ground level.

A mitigation strategy which relies on a covering regime can use the following approach: existing soils may be left *in situ* but all engineering techniques are confined to a level above-ground surface. Though the site will be covered by construction activities, this is effectively an avoidance strategy, for example hardstanding, landscaping or foundation elements are placed on top of, or suspended above, the undisturbed ground surface. The role of avoidance in an engineered mitigation strategy is very important as it can include the relocation of construction elements away from sensitive areas (eg moving basements or lift shafts to areas of previous disturbance). In addition, though not necessarily desirable, the process of field evaluation may archaeologically sterilise areas that can then be incorporated into an avoidance mitigation strategy.

If construction activities are to be located above the *in situ* archaeology, either there must be no construction impact on the archaeological deposits, or it must be confined within an archaeologically devoid or sterilised layer at the surface (eg topsoil). The devoid layer will act as a buffer between the new development and underlying deposits. Alternatively, a material could be introduced above the archaeological deposits to act as a buffer zone, either in place of or in addition to an archaeologically devoid surface material.

Two specific examples that illustrate the introduction of a new material to effectively isolate *in situ* archaeological remains at a site from surface construction activities include covering by water of the Late Bronze Age site at Flag Fen in Peterborough (Figure 23) and covering of the Globe Theatre site in London with a chemically inert silica sand and load-spreading geogrid (Figure 24) (HTS 1996).

A number of studies have been conducted into the use of introduced materials to cover or backfill archaeological sites. Though very much conducted on a site-specific basis, the various studies have assessed the loading, hydrological and contamination impact of introducing foreign materials on to

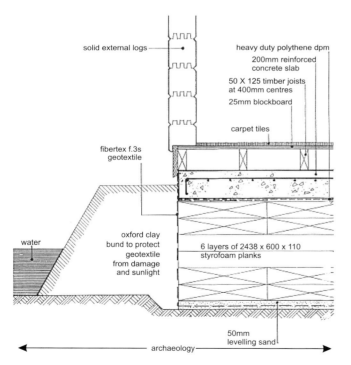

Figure 23 Engineered mitigation strategy to permit construction of a timber visitor centre above a Late Bronze Age platform at Flag Fen, Peterborough (After T Holmes)

Figure 24 Engineered mitigation strategy involving placement of sand above remains of the Globe Theatre, London (Photo: Hunting Technical Services)

the archaeology, and also the role which the materials can have in reintroducing or modifying the burial environment of a site. The information available on the backfilling of archaeological sites has been reviewed in the bibliography included with this report (Appendix D).

The reintroduction of burial conditions that promote archaeological preservation may be necessary if construction activities have caused an unavoidable or accidental disturbance of the ground. Though the reintroduction rather than maintaining of a burial environment is on the whole undesirable, it can be a valid objective of a mitigation strategy in specific cases. For example, at the Rose Theatre site in London the establishment of an irrigation system has reintroduced and now maintains waterlogged conditions around the *in situ* archaeological remains (English Heritage 1994) (Figure 25).

Covering systems can also act to discourage the unauthorised use of metal detectors to locate buried metal artefacts, by removing the remains from the detecting range of the instruments. Brass and galvanised steel chaff can also be added to

backfill materials to create excessive background 'noise' for metal detectors, preventing the detection of metal artefacts (Nielsen 1993).

4.4 Monitoring of mitigation strategies

The correct installation and maintenance of any mitigation strategy is vital if it is to perform its designed function of reducing construction impact on archaeological remains. To ensure this is achieved the establishment of a monitoring programme may be necessary, in which the following two issues may be addressed.

Firstly, there needs to be confirmation that the mitigation strategy was installed correctly. This can involve checking that approved materials were used in the designed manner and at the correct stage of the project. If a deviation from the approved methodology has occurred, the revisions should be agreed and monitored to ensure that the mitigation strategy is still able to perform as designed. Once installed, monitoring of the structural stability of the mitigation strategy may also be necessary (Figure 26). Flexibility and the ability to revise elements of the mitigation strategy are important given the frequently unpredictable nature of development projects; for example, unfore-

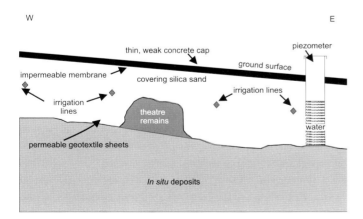

Figure 25 Covering mitigation strategy installed over the Rose Theatre remains, London (Adapted from English Heritage 1994)

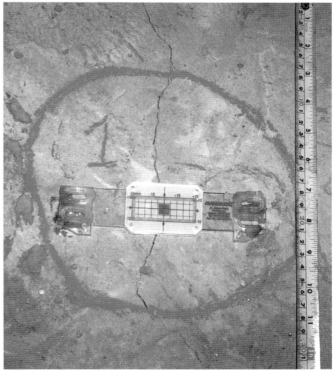

Figure 26 Monitoring of cracks within the covering mitigation strategy installed above the Rose Theatre remains, London (Photo: Hunting Technical Services)

seen ground conditions, adverse weather and equipment fail- ures all contribute to delays and revisions in a project. A watch- ing brief conducted by a suitably trained professional should enable this form of monitoring to be undertaken.

Secondly, effectiveness of the mitigation strategy needs to be monitored to ensure the objective of *in situ* preservation of archaeological remains is being achieved. This can be achieved by the collection and interpretation of data on the *in situ* ground conditions and burial environment surrounding the archaeo- logical remains. The data can be obtained using a range of specialist monitoring devices, many of which were developed by either the agricultural or engineering professions (Figure 27). In recent years, many have been successfully applied to archae- ological sites on which *in situ* preservation is an issue, and a useful discussion of these devices was presented at the 1996 conference on *Preserving archaeological remains* in situ (Davis 1998). Establishment of a monitoring programme is important because it enables any failings in a mitigation strategy to be identified at the earliest occasion, and this then allows remedial

measures to be put in place before a site's burial environment becomes seriously altered.

A further approach to site monitoring may be the introduc- tion and assessment of control samples of archaeologically similar material. For example, knowledge gained from the study of decay rates in cotton strips and wood samples placed within *in situ* archaeological deposits could be used to assess the effec- tiveness of an archaeological mitigation strategy (Bell et al 1996). Additional information on the adoption of site-monitor- ing strategies can be obtained by reference to the bibliography provided with this study (Appendix D).

4.5 Summary conclusions

This study is intended to act as an information source to assist in the decision processes made by all professionals involved in the preservation of archaeological remains *in situ*. This should result in the development of improved site-management plans and the adoption of appropriate mitigation strategies, both of which will prevent the often avoidable destruction of the archaeological resource through construction or excavation.

A 'mitigation strategy' usually comprises a coordinated sequence of mitigation options aimed at avoiding or minimising the impact of construction activities on the archaeological remains at a site. Frequently the strategy will comprise a number of components including avoidance (by relocation), an engineered solution, limited or localised excavation, and a watching brief to satisfy the requirements of the planning condition. Whichever mitigation strategy is adopted, it should have a design life that will ensure its effectiveness for the life- span of the new development.

Ultimately, if there is to be a reasonable level of success in preserving archaeological remains *in situ*, there has to be a more intrinsic relationship between the constituent parties of the development team: that is, the developer/promoter, engineer, architect, archaeologist and the various groundworks and construction contractors. The establishment of monitored engi- neered mitigation strategies has been an important step towards this aim, but more research work is essential to enable effective and financially viable methods of preservation to be achieved.

More immediately, an improvement in the success of preserving archaeological remains can perhaps be achieved by improving the contact between engineers and archaeologists. Unfortunately it is still often the case that there is insufficient dialogue between developers, engineers and archaeologists at a suitably early stage in a development. This report discusses the importance of involving an archaeologist at the earliest possible stage in a project, and certainly before any form of ground- intrusive works have started. This could possibly be achieved if an Environmental Impact Assessment (EIA) was requested of

Figure 27   Direct monitoring of the moisture content of in situ *archaeological deposits in York with a neutron probe (Photo: Hunting Technical Services)*

the developer as a first requirement to obtaining a planning consent for a proposed development. An improved level of communication should also assist in making the various parties involved in a project aware that they have a *common aim:* that of getting the development built to an agreed timescale but without unnecessary erosion of the archaeological importance of the site. Because the developer or promoter is in a position to set the overall environmental tone of a construction project they must have the knowledge, awareness and recognition of all environmental issues affecting the site. The information can generally be provided by, among others, planners, archaeologists, civil and structural engineers, environmental consultants, architects and landscape architects. These professionals will also be able to provide a link between the promoter and contractors, and the regulatory authorities.

By whatever mechanism a mitigation strategy is achieved, it must be reached by involvement from both the archaeological and engineering professions in an integrated manner, and not as a result of a series of independent steps. The discussions may avoid the adoption of overengineered project designs which, if

building regulations permit, can be redesigned to be less ground intrusive. Though each development will require a site-specific, and perhaps unique, mitigation strategy, the overall aim of all strategies should be the avoidance of all forms of ground disturbance. If total avoidance is not possible, it should be minimised (engineered mitigation strategy) and confined to an agreed and clearly defined zone (both spatially and vertically). This can be achieved by a combination of partial avoidance and an engineered mitigation strategy, both of which should be the subject of a site-monitoring programme to verify their installation and performance.

Finally, following completion of a construction project, there should be a commitment to publish and make available the mitigation strategy adopted (eg foundation solution) and if applicable the findings from a site-monitoring programme. In this way, and through an aligned programme of research, a greater understanding will hopefully be gained of available mitigation strategies, the character of burial environments, and the disturbances that may result from the impact of construction activities.

APPENDIX A: TECHNICAL APPENDIX OF ENGINEERING PROCESSES

A1.0 Stage1: Pre-construction investigation

A1.1 Techniques involving excavation

A1.1.1 Trial pits and trenches

Description: Pits are generally dug to a maximum depth of 4.5m, using a backacter excavator. Depths of 6m are achievable with 360-degree excavators, though plant costs are higher and they are not frequently used. The plan area of these pits is commonly kept to a minimum of c 4m long by 0.9m wide, though they can be extended in either direction as required. A trial pit extended to significant length becomes a trench. Pits are generally logged as they progress downwards, enabling archaeological examination if required. Entry of personnel into unsupported pits is not permitted below depths of 1.2m. Supported pits are usually open sheeted and braced with light-weight hydraulic props. The pit is generally infilled immediately after logging, with the excavated soil compacted in 300mm layers (Clayton et al 1995; BS 5930: 1999).

Trial pits and trenches permit the examination of the ground *in situ*, in order to determine soil structure. They enable the collection of disturbed samples of any size and can also yield very high-quality undisturbed samples in firm cohesive strata. Given the general speed, ease and low costs of their construction, allied to the quality of information they provide, trial pits and trenches form an important part of most ground investigations.

They are often the first approach to site investigations, though they have two major limitations: depth of pit is too limited for many purposes, in which case they must be supplemented with boreholes. Collapse of pits in granular and/or waterbearing strata can limit their usefulness in these conditions.

Disturbance of near-surface soils: Within the area of the trial pit itself disturbance of the soil is total. There is lesser disturbance to the surrounding area caused by penetration of the backacter's legs into the soil, by the storage and subsequent clearing of the arisings and, where applicable, by the discharge of water pumped from wet pits.

It is also significant that excavators used for trial pitting are routinely used for clearing access routes, both for themselves and for other items of plant. Ground disturbance and so impact to buried archaeology may therefore occur even before the commencement of the excavation.

Mitigation of ground disturbance: Ground disturbance will be kept to a minimum, and be largely confined to the area of excavation, if the trial pits are excavated carefully by trained machine operators who are using well-maintained equipment. The excavator should also be fitted with the correct tools to carry out the task required of it (eg narrow toothless bucket on a long-reach excavator for deep trial pits excavated above a thin buried archaeological layer).

In addition, archaeological supervision of the works provides the most used means of minimising unnecessary ground disturbance. Restriction of machine movement and operation during wet ground conditions will reduce near-surface ground disturbance.

Access routes for the excavator and other plant to reach the trial pit or trench should be precisely located (both on site plans and across the site) in order to avoid areas of archaeological sensitivity. If sensitive areas are crossed, the traffic of plant may be restricted to limit ground disturbance (eg size of plant and number of movements during a working day). Alternatively, the route may need to be constructed to avoid ground disturbance during plant movement (eg geotextiles to limit surface rutting and spread high point loads). The mitigation of construction impact from the creation and use of access routes is discussed further in Section A2.6.

The penetration of the machine's legs into the soil can be reduced by the use of steel load-spreading plates below the legs, and by the excavator operating on a temporary surface (eg geo-textile). Disturbances caused by the temporary storage of aris-ings can also be reduced if the arisings are placed on a tarpau-lin or boards laid on the ground – such a precaution is commonly used to protect lawns.

If groundwater is encountered, discharges can be amelio-rated by feeding it to a watercourse (if permitted by the Environment Agency) or to the mains drainage system (if permitted by the Local Authority), alternatively the discharge could be released as a spray rather than a concentrated flow.

A1.1.2 Shafts

Description: A borehole permitting man-entry that can be constructed with a large-diameter piling rig, which is usually crane-mounted. They are usually 1m or more in diameter and, once constructed, permit the *in situ* logging and testing of soils and weak rocks and the taking of samples. Though very high-quality information can be obtained, they are very rare due to the cost of excavating a shaft. Also, they cannot be used in unstable soils or granular soils below the water table (Clayton et al 1995; BS 5930: 1999).

Disturbance of near-surface soils: The disturbance of the soils within the shaft will be total. Around the shaft and along the access route compression of the soil is to be expected due to the weight of the plant.

Mitigation of ground disturbance: Spreading of the load imposed by the boring rig will reduce ground compression. If the plant is motorised it is usually tracked, and therefore rutting of the soil will be less of a problem than with wheeled plant.

A1.1.3 Hand augers

Description: A manual method of forming boreholes of moderate diameter (up to *c* 150mm) to moderate depth (up to 6m). The equipment consists of one of a series of augering heads mounted on sectional rods at the upper end of which is a T-bar by which one or two personnel apply the necessary torque and downward thrust.

During construction the boreholes may be used for the purposes of soil logging and sampling and, once completed, for the installation of shallow instrumentation.

Though hand augers can be used in areas of limited or restricted access, and their construction in terms of equipment and personnel requirements is relatively inexpensive, they generally form a minor part of many ground investigations. This is because hand augers are frequently unable to penetrate the stony and compacted ground commonly found on urban development sites. Also, they cannot be used in granular soils below the water table, and the full range of auger bits are rarely held by site investigation contractors. Progress using hand augers is therefore frequently slow (Clayton et al 1995; BS 5930: 1999).

Disturbance of near-surface soils: Disturbance within the excavation is total, otherwise there is negligible disturbance.

Mitigation of ground disturbance: Ground disturbance is kept to a minimum by using trained operators, who are also aware of any archaeological constraints on the site. The work may need to be conducted by an archaeologist, or alternatively be supervised by them during a watching brief. This point is obviously applicable to all engineering techniques used during the site development.

A1.1.4 Light cable percussion boring (shell and auger boring)

Description: The formation of boreholes by repeatedly dropping one of a series of hollow cylindrical tools into the ground and thereby removing a plug of soil.

The plant used consists of a demountable tripod rig towed behind a Land Rover or similar vehicle, and the tools are lifted by means of a winch operating on the tripod rig. To aid progress through granular soils above the water table a water bowser may sometimes be in attendance. Where borehole positions are on a slope a scaffolding platform may be required.

Boreholes are commonly excavated to between 10m and 40m depth, although depths in excess of 100m can be achieved under suitable conditions. The borehole itself is most commonly between 150mm and 250mm diameter. Often an inspection pit will be excavated at the borehole site to check for services (water, gas, telephone, etc). Such a pit would be dug at most urban sites, and typically measure *c* 1m x 1m, and be 1.2m deep. The boreholes enable the collection of disturbed samples of small to moderate size, and undisturbed samples (in cohesive soils) of moderate quality, for the purposes of strata description and physical/chemical laboratory testing. Groundwater observations are made during boring and these can be supplemented by the installation of permanent monitoring instrumentation.

The borehole is backfilled on completion either with the arisings, or with a slurried mixture of cement and bentonite clay (a natural sodium montmorillonite clay mineral). Backfilling has the dual purpose of preventing future subsidence around boreholes due to their collapse and reforming any aquicludes which may exist within the soil sequence. This latter is most important to safeguard confined aquifers used for water supply, and to prevent problems due to groundwater ingress at the construction stage in projects such as deep basement construction and tunnelling. Bentonite or cement slurry achieves these objectives most effectively and is therefore often preferred despite increased cost. Simple instrumentation may be installed in a minority of boreholes and this is visited for monitoring regularly after completion of the ground investigation.

The plant used is robust and simple, and it forms an economical method of excavating deep boreholes through most soils and weak rocks encountered in the UK. Therefore, on suitable ground, light cable percussion boring is the most common means of excavating exploratory boreholes during a ground investigation.

The principal limitation of this method is access, as it cannot be used in conditions of very low headroom (though limited-headroom rigs are available). Additionally the standard rig cannot readily penetrate significant thickness of rock (Clayton et al 1995; BS 5930: 1999).

Disturbance of near-surface soils: The working area around the rig can be expected to cover an area of 5m x 10m, and parts of this area may become waterlogged if water is struck in the borehole. Soils within the inspection pit and borehole itself are completely disturbed. In wet conditions on unpaved surfaces bogging down of the plant on the access route to the borehole position can lead to severe rutting, and in drier weather compaction of frequently used access routes can occur. The compaction may be removed by subsoiling or 'ripping', which will physically disturb the soil profile. Backfilling of the borehole with bentonite/cement slurry may locally alter the chemical regime within the soil.

Mitigation of ground disturbance: Channelling away of any water brought to the surface and boarding over the working area will help to minimise ground disturbance around the borehole. Temporary trackways can be used on the access routes to avoid rutting, but these are expensive and the selection of a route to avoid sensitive areas is probably the best solution to this problem in the majority of cases. If all risk of chemical contamination of the soil is to be avoided then backfilling of the borehole with washed sand, at least over the sensitive part of its length, may be appropriate. However, the integrity of aquicludes within the soil sequence should be taken into account when specifying a backfill.

A1.1.5 Power auger

Description: A powered short-flight or continuous-flight helical auger, the stem of which may be solid or hollow and may be segmental.

Power augers can excavate small- or moderate-diameter boreholes, from which disturbed samples and small undisturbed samples for strata identification and limited laboratory testing can be recovered. They are, however, a secondary means of ground investigation in the UK, less commonly used than cable percussion boring and trial pits. This is because they are not as adaptable and offer few advantages over light cable percussion equipment, and therefore they are generally not cost-effective. Their principal advantage over other techniques is the speed of forming a borehole, and then they may come into their own on very specific tasks, for example probing of pile positions. However, this speed is at the expense of obtaining a detailed profile log. Small portable power augers may be used where restricted access (they can be hand-portable) or budget constraints prevent the use of larger plant.

Small rigs are, however, only suitable for small-diameter boreholes (up to c 100mm) of limited depth. Only 38mm undisturbed samples or larger-diameter but totally disturbed samples can be taken. Penetration is difficult through stiff or gravelly soils (Clayton et al 1995; BS 5930: 1999).

Disturbance of near-surface soils: Disturbance is usually limited to the actual borehole itself (and the inspection pit if such is required).

Mitigation of ground disturbance: As for hand augers, see Section 1.1.3.

A1.1.6 Rotary drilling (open hole)

Description: The formation of a borehole by rotary drilling methods in which no solid samples are taken during drilling. The material at the base of the hole is ground up by the drill bit and brought to the surface as a suspension within a flush fluid. Flush fluids in common use are air, water, mud and foam. Polymer muds are the most common flush fluid presently in use; many are biodegradable. Boreholes are backfilled with a slurry of cement and bentonite clay after completion.

Commonly employed in rock and some very stiff soils, they are used to form a borehole down which *in situ* tests may be performed, or which may be continued by other excavation methods once a stratum of interest is encountered.

It is a very rapid means of forming a borehole in soil or weak rock, and rotary drilling is the only ground-investigation method for forming a borehole in strong rock. The method generally requires heavy plant and the large rotary drilling rigs are often lorry-mounted. If ground conditions permit, smaller trailer or skid-mounted rigs and tracked rigs are also available. Additional plant may include a compressor and/or water bowser and possibly mixing and settlement tanks. The requirement for large and specialist equipment makes this method of ground investigation expensive. Its effectiveness is reduced when penetrating gravels (Clayton et al 1995; BS 5930: 1999).

Disturbance of near-surface soils: The working area can become waterlogged. Additives in flush fluids may enter the soil around the borehole to a limited degree. Access along unpaved routes can produce severe rutting in wet weather, and clearance of vegetation, etc may be required through overgrown areas. Otherwise disturbance is limited to the borehole itself and the inspection pit if such is required.

Mitigation of ground disturbance: The use of a flush fluid other than air or water reduces the likelihood of the working area becoming waterlogged. Mud flushes are recycled, foam flush has a low water content, and both discourage groundwater entry into the borehole by blocking off fissures and permeable strata. Similarly chemical contamination by flush additives will be inhibited by the formation of a 'cake' around the borehole wall so restricting the exchange of fluids between the soil and the borehole. The additives are also chemically inactive; mud consists for the most part of bentonite which is a naturally occurring clay mineral, while the foam is composed of long-chain polymers that biodegrade to stable organic compounds. The provision of temporary trackways will limit the potential for rutting of access routes but, as noted previously, these are expensive and rarely used. The intelligent choice of access routes, avoiding sensitive areas, is often a more suitable solution.

A1.1.7 Rotary drilling (coring)

Description: The formation of a borehole by rotary drilling methods in which a length of continuous core is taken during drilling. The annulus between the core and the borehole wall is ground up by the drill bit and brought to the surface as a suspension within a flush fluid. Core lengths are most commonly 1.5m or 3.0m. The standard core diameters used in ground investigation range from *c* 20mm to 165mm, though commonly used sizes lie within the range 41mm to 112mm. The larger diameters are used for coring weak or fractured materials. Boreholes are backfilled with a slurry of cement and bentonite clay after completion.

This method of drilling is commonly used in rock and some very stiff soils to obtain core samples, so enabling logging of the strata and laboratory testing. *In situ* tests can be performed in the borehole. Instruments can be installed in the completed borehole for the measurement of groundwater levels (among other things), as observations made during drilling are generally unreliable.

As with the open-hole drilling, this other form of rotary drilling is the only method of forming a borehole in strong rock. Unlike open-hole drilling, the coring of weak rock and very stiff clays can yield undisturbed samples (ie core) of a high quality. The method again requires fairly heavy plant, is expensive, and progress through gravels can be difficult. Recovery of the core in loose or gravelly soils can also be a problem (Clayton et al 1995; BS 5930: 1999).

Disturbance of near-surface soils: If water is struck in the borehole then the working area can become waterlogged. Access along unpaved routes can produce severe rutting in wet weather. Otherwise disturbance is limited to the borehole itself and the inspection pit if such is required. Limited chemical disturbance may arise from the cement/bentonite backfill, or from flushwater additives ('mud' or 'foam'); however, such materials are designed not to permeate the surrounding ground.

Mitigation of ground disturbance: As for open-hole rotary, see Section A1.1.6.

A1.1.8 Delft sampler

Description: A continuous sampler comprising a hollow tube which is pushed into the ground, enabling a cylinder of soil to rise up inside it. The soil cylinder is 66mm in diameter and can be as long as 19m in soft soils. The sampler is usually operated from a 10 tonne or 17 tonne static cone penetration truck.

The sampler permits a long sample of soft soils to be recovered that shows the continuous soil sequence. It is, however, very rarely used in the UK as thick sequences of soft soil are rarely encountered on development sites and the technique is unsuitable to the strong often gravelly soils in the UK (Clayton et al 1995; BS 5930: 1999).

Disturbance of near-surface soils: Little disturbance is caused, except for the area penetrated by the sampler.

Mitigation of ground disturbance: Where rutting of the soil is likely to occur, temporary trackways can be used; however, these are expensive and selection of an insensitive access route will be a preferable option in many cases.

A1.1.9 Window sampler

Description: An open-ended tube of between 40mm and 80mm diameter and up to 3m in length is driven into the ground by means of a high-frequency percussion hammer acting at the top of stiff connecting rods. The tube is withdrawn from the soil with a continuous sample retained within it. Apertures, or windows, in the tube permit the examination of the sample.

Used with increasing frequency on low-cost ground investigations this method can provide a continuous profile of the ground, from which disturbed samples can be recovered for laboratory testing. The system uses hand-portable equipment that can form boreholes in a rapid and economical manner, often in areas of limited access. Once formed, the borehole can then be used to install a range of instrumentation, such as groundwater-monitoring devices. The disadvantages of the system are: penetration is generally limited to 5–10m; the sample may not be retained in the tube in some ground conditions; and the samples are disturbed (Clayton et al 1995; BS 5930: 1999).

Disturbance of near-surface soils: Disturbance is usually limited to the formation of the hole.

Mitigation of ground disturbance: Not usually required.

A1.2 Techniques involving probing

A1.2.1 Static cone penetration test

Description: A cone of *c* 35mm diameter is jacked into the ground at a rate of $20mms^{-1}$. Resistance to the progress of the cone, and to the progress of a cylinder of similar diameter mounted concentrically behind the cone, is monitored and yields physical soil parameters. The equipment used is commonly mounted within an enclosed truck of *c* 10–17 tonnes gross weight in order to provide reaction to the cone. A lighter system relies on screw pickets to provide this reaction.

The test is a widely used method of investigation in soft and firm soils due to its speed of operation. A range of physical soil parameters can be determined, and penetration is possible to depths of 20m or more. For example, the test is particularly useful in establishing the profile of a competent soil buried beneath a softer material. However, no samples are recovered, confirmation of strata by boring and sampling methods is recommended, and some important soil parameters cannot be determined (Meigh 1987).

Disturbance of near-surface soils: Cone penetration holes are usually not backfilled. As there are no arisings and no flush system, disturbance to the ground is limited to the passage of the vehicle and the formation of the hole.

Mitigation of ground disturbance: Not generally required; rutting of access routes may be avoided by using temporary trackways, but a choice of access route through an insensitive area is more economical.

A1.2.2 Dynamic cone penetration test

Description: The dynamic cone apparatus is a lightweight, even portable, rig with which a cone progresses vertically through the soil as a result of repeated hammer blows delivered to the cone from the surface via stiff rods. This inexpensive test produces a profile with depth of the number of blows required to penetrate a given distance.

It is not in common use as the information yielded is inadequate for most ground investigations; however, it can be useful in delineating the boundary between a weak soil overlying a stronger stratum. Its other main uses are at sites where access is severely restricted or where basic information is required. There have also been a variety of tools in use, and therefore the energy of the hammer and dimensions of the cone are non-standard making interpretation difficult. However, standardisation is well advanced and two versions are now included in the British Standard (BS 1377: 1990).

Disturbance of near-surface soils: The equipment produces little disturbance beyond the formation of a small-diameter hole. An inspection pit may be required.

Mitigation of ground disturbance: Care in use of the equipment rig to avoid ground disturbance outside the area directly affected by the cone.

A1.3 Techniques in preformed excavations

A1.3.1 Standard penetration tests

Description: A hollow steel cylinder with a tapered cutting shoe (termed the split spoon sampler) is driven into the soil at the base of an existing borehole by means of a hammer of standard mass falling through a standard distance. The number of blows required to drive the split spoon sampler 300 mm, after bedding in, is recorded and can be correlated with a wide range of physical soil parameters.

The test determines some soil parameters and is used to retrieve a small disturbed sample from a pre-drilled borehole. It is a very simple and inexpensive *in situ* test for use in all soil types, and it is used repeatedly in virtually all cable percussion boreholes and also in rotary boreholes.

It is especially useful in granular soils which are not amenable to undisturbed sampling, but its performance needs care in waterbearing granular soils. The test also relies on empirical correlation rather than direct measurement of fundamental soil parameters, requiring a degree of experience when interpreting the data (BS 1377: 1990).

Disturbance of near-surface soils: It is not used in isolation and has no impact on the ground beyond that of the associated excavations used to form the borehole.

Mitigation of ground disturbance: None is required.

A1.3.2 Field vane tests

Description: A four-bladed cruciform vane attached by means of stiff rods to a torque head. Occurs in several forms from a 'pocket' version, to a larger machine which is two-person portable. When it is pushed into a cohesive soil and the blades then turned, a cylinder of soil is sheared. Measurement of the torque on the rod yields a value for the undrained strength of the soil, and this gives a strength of soft soils which are difficult to sample adequately for laboratory testing.

The hand-held version is used for strength assessment in trial pits, while the larger vanes may be used at the bottom of an existing borehole, or pushed directly into soft soils from the surface.

Though this portable test is inexpensive and quick, it induces soil deformations which are not fully understood and this can lead to results at variance from those obtained by conventional laboratory testing (BS 1377: 1990).

Disturbance of near-surface soils: Very little disturbance unless used in a pre-drilled hole in which case the disturbance is that associated with the boring method.

Mitigation of ground disturbance: There is little option for mitigation of ground disturbance caused by use of the vane itself.

A1.3.3 Pressuremeter test

Description: There are a number of different kinds of pressuremeter equipment; the most commonly used in the UK is the Cambridge Self Boring Pressuremeter (SBPM). The Cambridge SBPM is a cylindrical tool c 80mm in diameter and a metre or so long. At its lower end there is a cutting shoe enabling the device to drill itself into the ground when attached to the drill rods of a standard rotary drilling rig. Above the cutting shoe there is a membrane occupying the entire circumference of the tool. Pressuremeters work by causing surfaces attached to the apparatus (in this case the membrane) to move outwards and distort the soil or weak rock with which the apparatus is in contact. The force imposed, and the resulting deformation, are measured and yield a value for the shear modulus of the soil, and can yield an estimate of the *in situ* lateral stress.

The pressuremeter is a soil-testing device that has until recently primarily been used as a research tool. However, there has been a growing commercial use of the test on prestige projects.

The test is used because it produces high-quality results from *in situ* soils; furthermore, the shear modulus is difficult to measure accurately in any other way and the test is capable of measuring small-strain behaviour of soils. In soft ground the self-boring action works adequately; however, in the majority of soils found in the UK it proves necessary to assist the SBPM using standard rotary drilling techniques. The test is expensive and interpretation of the measurements must be undertaken by skilled engineers (Mair and Wood 1987).

Disturbance of near-surface soils: Little impact beyond that of the drilling operation.

Mitigation of ground disturbance: Not required once the borehole has been formed.

A1.3.4 Plate-loading test

Description: An *in situ* test in which a horizontal soil surface is prepared, either in a fully supported trial pit or, deeper, in a shaft, and then loaded by means of a rigid plate jacked off an immovable kentledge at the ground surface (BS 1377: 1990).

Though an expensive form of ground investigation, due to the associated costs of excavating a pit or shaft and providing kentledge, the test can provide high-quality data on the stiffness and strength of the soil. Data can also be obtained on the ultimate bearing capacity of the soil (Mair and Wood 1987).

Disturbance of near-surface soils: Very little disturbance beyond that associated with forming the excavation and erecting the kentledge (which typically will require a crane). However, ground compaction will occur beneath the plate during the test and below the kentledge.

Mitigation of ground disturbance: As discussed for trial pits, see Section A1.1.1.

A1.3.5 Permeability tests (soakage test)

Description: Permeability tests are typically carried out in pre-drilled boreholes below the equilibrium water table. Water is either injected into, or removed from, the hole and the rate at which equilibrium conditions are recovered gives an indication of soil or rock permeability. An associated test is the soakage or soakaway test, which is carried out in a small near-surface pit, above the water table. This latter test is used to assist in the design of soakaways, for example on contracts where on-site disposal of surface water run-off is required as part of the final, or temporary, works design.

Disturbance of near-surface soils: The soakaway test is the only reliable method of establishing the required parameters for soakaways and it requires the excavation of a pit, which completely disturbs the soils within the pit. The test generally uses a large volume of water and so the soils surrounding the pit are then saturated. Changes in moisture content of archaeological deposit may occur.

Mitigation of ground disturbance: As with all engineering operations, the ground conditions in which the test will be performed should be carefully evaluated before its use is permitted. This is because the introduction or removal of water from archaeological deposits is potentially damaging to its *in situ* preservation. During the actual test, collapse of pit sides should be prevented by shoring where applicable.

A1.4 Geophysical surveying techniques

Description: Geophysical techniques are based on determining variations in a physical property of the ground remotely. Surface geophysical surveying techniques may be divided into passive and active techniques. Passive techniques such as self-potential, gravimetric and magnetometry detect the spatial differences in properties of the ground, resulting in a measured anomaly which must then be interpreted. Active techniques, such as electrical resistivity, ground conductivity, ground-penetrating radar and seismic, measure particular events caused by an input, and during interpretation these measurements are converted into properties. Downhole geophysical logging techniques may also be used to provide depth profiles of strata and groundwater properties. Available techniques include resistivity, conductivity, sonic, gamma, neutron, fluid velocity and temperature logs.

Most of the techniques locate only some form of anomaly where the materials on either side of it have some markedly different physical properties. Such anomalies may occur, for example, at the boundary between two fill materials, saturated and unsaturated materials, underground services, cavities or buried archaeological structures. They will be used on sites where a strong anomaly is expected from a particular target or feature, or where interpolation of subsurface detail is required between boreholes or trial pits (BS 5930: 1999).

Disturbance of near-surface soils: With non-contacting techniques disturbance of the ground is minimal, and the equipment is often light enough to be carried by a single person. Resistivity and seismic methods require the sensors to be in direct contact with the ground. However, soil disturbance is confined to surface deposits at the point of each sensor, and damage will normally be negligible.

Downhole logging methods generally do not require contact with the borehole wall to work (apart from calliper logs), and therefore will not cause any physical disturbance of the soil. Seismic methods may require the borehole to first be filled with water, which could create an impact on previously dry archaeological deposits. The disturbance caused by the borehole construction is described in Section A1.1.

Mitigation of ground disturbance: The need to traffic over a site can require the avoidance of work during wet conditions. Due to their low impact on *in situ* archaeological remains, geophysical techniques can act as a useful first stage in a ground investigation; however, their often ambiguous results mean they are not used in isolation by an engineer.

A2.0 Stage 2: Pre-construction activities

A2.1 Topsoil stripping and vegetation clearance

Description: The surface vegetation is stripped first and burned or disposed off site. On small sites trees, bushes, etc can usually be 'grubbed out' using hand tools but on larger sites mechanised plant may be justified.

The topsoil is then stripped to a maximum depth of *c* 300mm, again using a bulldozer or mechanical shovel on sites where such plant is economically justified. The soil is stored on site for reuse or disposed off site. Due to its compressibility and weakness (caused largely by its organic content), this stripping of topsoil is considered essential beneath earthworks, temporary and permanent roads, and ground-bearing foundations (Chudley and Greeno 2001).

Disturbance of near-surface soils: Scraping away of shallow-rooted surface vegetation and topsoil can be carried out accurately by a skilled operator using even the heaviest items of plant. However, damage to the underlying ground may still occur due to rutting under wheeled plant and compaction under heavy-tracked plant on soft soils, and due to the grubbing out of deep-rooted vegetation. Though the level of disturbance to the topsoil and subsoil will vary depending on the scale of operations, it is an unavoidable occurrence.

Mitigation of ground disturbance: Rutting and compaction of the underlying strata can be reduced by careful plant selection and by working in the dry summer months when soils will be stronger. Depending on the form of the later development, it may be permissible to remove roots manually to a limited depth, leaving the remainder *in situ*. Careful mapping of the soil resources to produce management plans will assist in confining the soil-stripping operation to areas and depths of least archaeological sensitivity. Archaeological supervision during the soil stripping will then verify that the management plan is carried out as agreed, and that unexpected remains are dealt with by a trained professional.

During site clearance the involvement of an archaeologist is important because the work is usually conducted quickly and it can result in large areas of the site being disturbed.

A2.2 Remediation of site contamination

Description: As a result of past industrial or mining activities, or from the tipping and disposal of waste, unacceptable concentrations of substances (in solid, liquid or gaseous form) may be present on a site proposed for development. Guidance on the identification and investigation of potentially contaminated sites is given in the British Standards Code of Practice (BS 10175: 2001). The general procedure adopted is similar to that used for a geotechnical or ground investigation, though the sampling strategy and sample analysis are designed from a contamination rather than an engineering perspective (CIRIA 1995a–b).

If required, remediation of contamination on a site is generally conducted using one or more of the following approaches:

1   Excavation and then total removal of the material containing the contamination for disposal, using conventional civil-engineering techniques. For example, excavator and dump truck for on-site or more likely off-site disposal to landfill.

2   Excavation, treatment and then replacement of material using a combination of conventional engineering techniques (ie approach 1) and *ex situ* treatment processes. The *ex situ* processes can involve similar techniques to those employed during the *in situ* treatment of contaminated material (see approach 3), as well as the following examples:

   i) particle segregation (eg excavated soils or other materials are physically screened or washed above ground to remove contaminated materials before the remaining 'clean' material is returned to the site)

   ii) pump-and-treat (eg excavated boreholes are used to pump contaminated groundwater for above-ground treatment using carbon sorption, air stripping, chemical treatment/precipitation etc. The treated groundwater may then be discharged back to the ground)

3   *In situ* based treatments involve the application of physical, chemical or biological processes to either remove, destroy or modify contaminants within the subsurface environment. Such treatment methods rely on a variety of 'natural' or 'engineered' processes to achieve remediation, which are summarised below:

   iii) thermal (eg steam and hot-air stripping, radio-frequency heating and vitrification)

   iv) volatilisation (eg application of a vacuum or air injection/sparging to a borehole and then recovery of volatile organic contaminants)

   v) physical (eg soil washing and electrokinetic)

   vi) chemical (eg *in situ* leaching and soil flushing)

   vii) biological (eg land farming with contaminant-tolerant

species (phytoremediation) and *in situ* bioremediation)

viii) soilidification/stabilisation (eg cement-based or lime-based pozzolans, hydraulic slags, thermoplastics, organophilic clays)

4 Containment systems that use in-ground barriers to physically isolate a contaminated mass of ground from the surrounding media (soil or water). Barriers may include both a surface cover (eg topsoil, clean inert material or a concrete or similar hard cover) and a vertical in-ground barrier. The engineering operations typically associated with vertical barriers are similar to those employed during ground improvement and groundwater-control operations (Section A2.12 and A2.13), and they include:

i) displacement systems (eg sheet piling, vibrated beam wall, membrane wall)

ii) excavated barriers (eg scant wall, concrete diaphragm, shallow cut-off wall, slurry trench wall)

iii) injection barriers (eg chemical grouting, jet grouting and mixing, auger mixing)

iv) other systems (eg chemical barrier, ground freezing, biobarriers, electrokinetic barriers).

Details of the above approaches for the remediation of contamination are discussed in a useful series of 12 reports from the Construction Industry Research and Information Association (CIRIA 1995).

Disturbance of near-surface soils: Depending on the technique employed, the remediation of contamination may affect the physical, chemical or biological character of the ground. Because the removal (for disposal or *ex situ* treatment) or containment of contaminated ground generally involves conventional civil-engineering techniques, the potential ground disturbances have been described in Section A1.1, and Sections A2.12 to A2.13 respectively. The construction activities described in these sections are primarily those associated with excavation, ground improvement and groundwater control.

Though still relatively uncommon in England, the *in situ* methods of remediation may cause a significant impact on *in situ* archaeological remains. This is because the ground disturbance caused during remediation is commonly concentrated within the near-surface soils, in which both the contaminants and archaeological remains are typically located. The impacts may result from the physical moving of soil during soil washing, introduction of chemicals during soil flushing, increase or change of micro-organisms populations during bioremediation, or heating and fusing of the ground during soilidification/stabilisation.

Mitigation of ground disturbance: Mitigation of disturbances caused by excavation during the remediation of site contamination can be undertaken using the same approaches as described for a ground investigation (Section A1.1). The miti-

gation of containment systems can be achieved by the adoption of measures relevant to the type of in-ground barrier that will be used in the remediation process (eg mitigation of grouting).

If *in situ* remediation methods are proposed, there should be an assessment of its potential impact on the site's *in situ* archaeological remains, both within and surrounding the contaminated ground. If a risk to the archaeological remains is identified, it may be possible to limit the depth of *in situ* remediation to near-surface soil layers only, or to require the physical isolation of archaeological remains from the ground to be treated (eg membrane containment). Alternatively, an avoidance mitigation strategy may be necessary in which the final development is redesigned to avoid the need for contamination remediation within the areas of archaeological sensitivity.

A2.3 Site security, hoardings and fencing

Description: Hoardings in the form of a close-boarded fence must be erected on a site adjacent to a public highway or footpath (Highways Act 1980). A permit to erect the hoarding must be obtained from the Local Authority. Hoardings are typically 2.4m high and will be supported on posts set at 1.5–2.0m centres, buried a minimum of *c* 750mm into cast *in situ* mass-concrete sockets of *c* 300mm diameter. Where required, the hoarding will be propped from within the site. The props will be anchored to stakes driven into the ground or set into concrete sockets as above.

Disturbance of near-surface soils: Ground disturbance will be associated with forming the holes to take the load-bearing posts. These will be dug either manually or with an auger. In the normal course of events disturbance around these sockets will be minimal. On completion of the development it may be a requirement to remove the buried concrete, and this can be achieved by pulling the posts bodily from the ground or by digging them out. In either case a degree of ground disturbance may be expected.

Mitigation of ground disturbance: Use of above-ground footings, possibly positioned on a temporary load-spreading surface, such as a geotextile laid on the soil surface. Also ensure archaeological supervision during erection of the fences if excavation is required.

A2.4 Protection of existing site features

Description: Features existing on the site may require protection from engineering operations during the development's construction, for example known archaeological remains, trees or existing buildings. Delineation of a 'safety zone' around the feature using lightweight fencing may be adequate; more robust protection would require foundation works similar to those of hoardings (see above).

Disturbance of near-surface soils: If secure fencing is required then the comments relating to hoardings above will be equally applicable here.

Mitigation of ground disturbance: Adopt the same mitigation options as for hoardings.

A2.5 Contractor accommodation and services

Description: The type of accommodation provided is at the discretion of the contractor and may range from a touring caravan to fully serviced mobile offices. If the offices fall under the Offices, Shops and Railway Premises Act 1963 then there are minimum requirements covering the floor-space and overall volume available to each regular occupant. In addition to office accommodation there may also be a requirement for first aid, eating, clothes-drying, washing and sanitary facilities. These requirements are governed by the Construction (Health and Welfare)(Amended) Regulations 1974.

The working accommodation is usually grouped in a single compound for ease of communication and security. Depending on the size of the site, mains services may be laid on and there may be a plant workshop and fuel stores. If there are vehicle-washing facilities on the site, as is usual for earthworks contracts, then large volumes of wastewater will be generated which will require drainage works.

Disturbance of near-surface soils: The majority of site offices will utilise either existing buildings or temporary 'porta-cabin' structures. Ground disturbance may result from the connection of below-ground services to the temporary buildings, which may require trenching to limited depth. Placement of a load on the ground could result in compaction, which may be severe and have associated rutting of the ground if the point load is high (eg beneath struts used to support portacabins). Inadequate water-disposal facilities (eg from gutters off buildings, sink overflows and wheel-washing facilities) could result in both flooding of the ground and surface erosion due to run-off.

Mitigation of ground disturbance: With the exception of drainage, services can usually be routed above ground or even overhead. Also, to avoid the need for trenching, existing service lines and drainage system should be used wherever possible. If trenching is necessary, the careful location of sanitary facilities, vehicle-washing plant, etc close to existing mains drains or cess tanks should reduce the requirement for long drainage runs.

An important mitigation option, applicable to many situations, is the early involvement of an archaeologist when determining accommodation and service requirements on the site.

A2.6 Access roads

Description: In cases where a final development includes roads or other areas of hardstanding, these will often be partially constructed early in the contract and used as the temporary site-access roads or storage areas. Access roads are laid after the removal of topsoil and vegetation and the digging out of soft-spots, replacing them with granular fill. A geotextile may then be laid on this prepared formation before well-graded stone or hard-core is spread and compacted (Watson 1994).

Disturbance of near-surface soils: Provided topsoil is left *in situ* and the roads are properly constructed under dry weather conditions, the disturbance should be limited to minor removal of soft-spots and possible compaction of the underlying soil by the road traffic. However, if the ground is wet and the road construction not sufficiently substantial then deep rutting can occur and stone or hard-core imported to improve the running surface may then be forced into the underlying soil to appreciable depth, maybe 1.5m or greater. Resulting disturbance to near-surface soils can be severe. The potential impact on underlying archaeology will be exacerbated if the road construction has also included removal of topsoil.

Once constructed, an access road may alter the water regime within the underlying and undisturbed ground. For example, if the road is constructed with an impermeable surface the moisture content of the soil beneath may remain effectively constant (drying by surface evaporation is prevented by the road, as is drainage down from the surface to the soil). Conversely, where lateral movement of subsurface water occurs, the soil under the road may become saturated unless roadside drainage is provided.

Mitigation of ground disturbance: Other than a watching brief, there is little scope for archaeological involvement during access-road construction. Therefore, at the planning stage, input from the archaeologists into the selection of access routes will be an important mitigation option.

Once the route and design criteria of each road are agreed, their careful construction in periods of dry weather will do much to reduce the risk of severe disturbance. The laying of a geotextile or geogrid reinforcement on the formation soil may avoid the need to dig out small soft-spots, and also reduce the degree of differential compaction of the formation soil. Drainage measures (eg permeable membranes or land drains) may be necessary to maintain the water regime in ground beneath and surrounding the road. Restrictions on the plant size and number of machine movements may be required to limit ground disturbance, and flexibility should be allowed for in case of adverse weather conditions and deteriorating ground conditions (eg poor surface drainage).

A2.7 Site storage

Description: The manner of site storage will depend on the size, value and susceptibility to weather exposure of the equipment or materials on site. Small items, portable valuable items or items susceptible to weathering will be kept in a lockable store or tool vaults. Bulk materials and large items such as vehicles may be stored in a lockable compound. This may be close-boarded and constructed in a similar way to hoardings, or fenced with chain-link; again the foundation requirements are similar to hoardings.

The site storage area is often adjacent to the accommodation area for added security.

Disturbance of near-surface soils: The loading imposed on the ground by stored materials can be significant, and may cause compaction or consolidation of soft near-surface soils. Greater ground disturbance may arise from the bulk storage of aggregate or cement in silos at an on-site batching plant, and this would normally require properly constructed foundations. The erection of secure compounds on the site will involve excavations to fix posts and hoardings, as described above. Contamination of the ground which may impact on buried archaeology can result from spillages of fuel or other chemicals, if these are stored on the site. Ground compaction is to be expected near the stores due to the volume of site traffic they will generate.

Mitigation of ground disturbance: Ground loading from stored materials can be limited by restricting the permitted height of stockpiles. It may be possible to construct secure compounds using methods which do not involve ground penetration or cause compaction, such as temporary working surfaces and load-spreading geogrids. Storage of fuel and other chemicals within containment structures can prevent ground contamination. Adequately constructed access roads will minimise the effects of trafficking.

A2.8 Shoring

Description: Shoring may be required to support the wall(s) of an existing structure when its lateral support has been removed. The shoring comprises a frame of timber or steel which rakes downwards from the supported wall to the ground where a pit is dug to achieve a sound bearing surface, sufficient to provide adequate reaction to the shoring frame.

Disturbance of near-surface soils: The digging of a pit in which to found the shoring frame is the most likely cause of ground disturbance.

Mitigation of ground disturbance: The depth of pit can be reduced by increasing its base area, though the depth is rarely great and mitigation may not be necessary. Point loads from the shoring may require inclusion of load-spreading devices (eg spreading plates and geotextiles) to minimise ground compaction.

A2.9 Pile probing

Description: After demolition on previously developed sites, new pile positions are often probed in order to check for obstructions (mainly old foundations) close to ground level. Usually the full depth of any made ground on the site is probed, and in a major urban setting this may involve probing to 6–8m. Any suitable available plant can be used, for example a back-acter is perhaps the most common for situations where the obstructions are likely to be shallow. Deeper obstructions can be identified using a truck-mounted auger and, if already on site, the piling rig may be used for probing.

Disturbance of near-surface soils: Ground disturbance in probed areas is extensive to the full depth of any made ground. If archaeological remains are present the impact of probing is likely to be high, and there is little or no scope for its assessment due to the absence of an exposed profile or recovery of soil samples.

Mitigation of ground disturbance: Non-intrusive methods, for example ground-probing radar (see Section A1.4), may be used in advance of probing within sensitive areas. The use of shallow excavations at the point of probing may also be necessary to avoid uncontrolled disturbance of any archaeological remains present.

A2.10 Trial piles

Description: Trial piles are constructed and tested prior to the main piling contract in order to check the design assumptions and construction method. Two or more trial piles of different length may be constructed in case of premature failure of the primary trial pile. Usually only one of these piles is tested. Testing involves the application of a load to the pile head and the measurement of the resulting deflection. A trial pile will be loaded to failure if this is within the capacity of the loading equipment, but in any case it is loaded to 300 per cent of design load. Most piles are designed to support vertical loads and they are therefore loaded vertically in test; some, however, are intended to support dominant horizontal loads and these will be loaded laterally.

Vertical load is applied by means of a hydraulic jack placed centrally on the pile head. Reaction to the jack is provided either by a steel framework which is anchored into the ground by three or more anchor piles, or by a number of heavy weights (kentledge) which are placed on a steel trestle over the pile head. The former method is often preferred from the view-points of both convenience and safety. In lateral load tests two piles are installed and these are either pulled together by a system of wire ropes, or jacked apart (Weltman 1980).

Disturbance of near-surface soils: There is little disturbance to the ground beyond that caused by the trial pile (and anchor pile) installation. Movements of the pile under test, even at failure, are small.

Mitigation of ground disturbance: For mitigation of ground disturbance during pile construction see Section A3.2.

A2.11 Tower crane bases

Description: Tower cranes are an essential feature of many medium- to large-size construction sites, and they comprise a swing jib or other crane mounted on top of a tower. There are no national standards relating to the design of tower crane foundations; however, they are subject to unusual loads, especially overturning forces, and therefore must be very firmly founded. The foundations of fixed tower cranes are of two types: either the crane is anchored into a large concrete block which may be piled or incorporated into the foundations of the building, or it has an extended cruciform base, the extremities of which are supported on piles, pads or a single large slab. To reduce the size of the foundation needed, tall cranes may be tied in to the building under construction.

Other types of tower crane are movable. Climbing cranes are founded within a completed part of the structure and are raised as the construction proceeds upwards. Travelling cranes are usually mounted on rails; these require very strong and stiff foundations (CIRIA 1996).

Disturbance of near-surface soils: The ground disturbance will be related to the foundation type selected for the crane base (see Section A3.0). The foundations will be designed to support the load imposed by both the crane and its operation, and the load may compact and so disturb the underlying ground.

Mitigation of ground disturbance: This relates to the particular foundation method chosen; mitigation options are described in Section A3.0.

Where it is particularly important to avoid ground disturbance then it may be possible to locate tower cranes away from sensitive areas (at the planning stage) and/or use mobile cranes.

Involvement of the archaeologist: Agreeing the location of tower and mobile cranes by both the engineer and archaeologist is an important mitigation option, and it should be undertaken at an early stage of the project. Once positioned, cranes enable enforcement of restricted access to archaeologically sensitive areas, while still permitting supply of construction equipment and materials to all permitted parts of the site.

A2.12 Ground improvement

A2.12.1 Introduction

Any process which results in an improvement in the strength or stiffness of a body of soil is termed ground improvement. Such an improvement of poor ground is often undertaken to enable the use of shallow rather than the more expensive deep foundations (Charles 1993; Bowles 1996).

The principal methods of ground improvement, the choice of which may depend on local conditions (eg access, archaeo-

logical remains, and presence nearby of vibration-sensitive buildings and services), are described in the following sections.

A2.12.2 Replacement

Description: Removal of the poor soil and either relaying it in compacted layers or replacing it with imported compacted fill. This method quickly becomes uneconomic on large sites or where poor ground is deep, unless a local source of cheap fill is available.

Disturbance of near-surface soils: The excavated soil will be totally disturbed.

Mitigation of ground disturbance: No mitigation of the disturbed area is possible, other than to follow the options listed for excavations during a ground investigation (Section A1.1).

A2.12.3 Surcharging (preloading)

Description: Loading of the soil to enforce consolidation settlement, thereby strengthening the soil and reducing the settlement of the final construction (after removal of the surcharge). The technique is only effective on soft clays and silts and relies largely on the expulsion of groundwater. It can take a long time (months or years), though the process can be accelerated by the installation of drains into the surcharged soil. Commonly used on highways projects where embankments cross alluvial plains.

Disturbance of near-surface soils: If construction of the surcharge is preceded by vegetation and topsoil stripping, physical ground disturbance may be extensive. This, and operations to place the first layers of surcharge fill, may also disturb the underlying soil due to trafficking of plant and heavy machines.

During surcharging, compression of the soil beneath the applied load will largely involve uniform volumetric strain rather than shear strains. Therefore, though archaeological deposits will be physically compressed, there should be little movement of remains from their position within the soil profile.

Mitigation of ground disturbance: In archaeologically sensitive areas geotextile reinforcement may be used to further reduce shear strains in the underlying soils. Use of such materials may also avoid the need for topsoil stripping in some cases.

A2.12.4 Dynamic compaction

Description: The dropping of heavy weights on to the soil from a great height in a grid pattern in order to effect deep compaction. The impact energies are high, for example a 15 tonne weight may be dropped through 20m. The method is most suitable for unsaturated granular soils and it is unsuitable for saturated cohesive soils. A crane is used to lift and drop the weight leading to substantial mobilisation costs. In addition there may be a need for a granular blanket to act as a working platform for the crane. A recent development is the rapid impact compactor in which a 7 tonne weight is dropped through 1.2m; the reduction in energy delivered per impact compared to the traditional system is partially compensated by a very much higher frequency of impacts. The mobilisation costs of this equipment are lower and there is less likelihood that a dedicated working platform will be required.

Disturbance of near-surface soils: Using either method, high levels of volumetric and shear strains are imposed on the soil and disturbance must be taken as total.

Mitigation of ground disturbance: If remains are within the ground to be improved, there are considered to be no mitigation options available to reduce the resulting impact from dynamic compaction.

A2.12.5 Vibrocompaction

Description: The densification of granular soil by the action of a vibrating poker inserted into the ground, a typical maximum depth of insertion is 6m. Water or compressed air is jetted into the ground through the nose of the poker to flush out loose material and ease the penetration of the poker. The method is not commonly used in the UK due to the unsuitability of the ground conditions here.

Disturbance of near-surface soils: At the point of poker insertion the disturbance will be total. There will then be a radial effect on the soil structure, decreasing with distance, as the poker vibrates.

Mitigation of ground disturbance: Within the ground affected by vibrocompaction mitigation of ground disturbance is not considered possible.

A2.12.6 Vibroplacement

Description: Similar to vibrocompaction but accompanied by the installation of columns of compacted stone or concrete into the soil. This factor extends the applicability of the method to cohesive soils, and this technique is therefore widely used in the UK. Compressed air is used in preference to water on most contracts due to the difficulty of disposing of large quantities of wastewater.

Disturbance of near-surface soils: Columns will generally be installed at spacings of just a few metres, therefore ground disturbance may be taken as total.

Mitigation of ground disturbance: Within the ground affected by vibroplacement, mitigation of ground disturbance is again not considered possible.

A2.12.7 Grouting

Description: Grouting is a technique of ground improvement in which a grouting fluid or slurry (either cement or chemical based) is injected via a series of boreholes with the purpose of permanently infilling voids and stiffening the soil. Varieties of chemical grout include bitumen and resins (eg epoxies, acrylic and phenolic aminoplastics), and they can be used for water-proofing as well as ground strengthening. Additives may also be used, for example bentonite to increase the grout's cohesion and viscosity, and calcium chloride to accelerate the grout's setting time (Henn 1996).

Four main approaches to grouting are described below:

1 Permeation grouting describes the technique of injecting low-viscosity grout which seeps through the voids between individual particles of soil or fragments of rock, eventually hardening to cement the entire body of soil or rock. Commonly used in dam foundations and tunnelling to reduce permeability, the technique also improves ground strength and stiffness. In coarse-grained soils such as coarse sand and gravel a cementitious grout consisting of cement, bentonite and water is used, perhaps with the addition of a filler such as pulverised fuel ash (fly ash) or fine sand if the pores are especially large. In fine-grained soils such as medium and fine sands ultrafine cement or chemical grouts are used.

2 Hydro fracture or compensation grouting describes a technique in which a fluid cement-based grout is injected under such pressure that it causes tensile failure of the ground. Cracks form, often in a horizontal plane, and radiate outwards from the injection borehole; these cracks fill with grout as they form. The effect is therefore to lift the overlying ground. This technique may be used to compensate for subsidence due to tunnelling in urban settings. An increase in the bearing capacity and shearing resistance of the soil also results.

3 Jet grouting is a technique in which a lance is introduced into the ground and rotated while fluid cement-based grout is jetted out horizontally at high pressure. This acts to loosen soil around the lance and mix it into a grout slurry. The effect is to form columns of grouted soil at any orientation within the ground or, if placed in a continuous line, forming a low-permeability and semi-structural wall below ground.

4 Compaction grouting is a method of ground improvement wherein a viscous cement-based grout is injected into the ground and expands as a body away from the point of injection. It uses high grouting pressures that effectively change the soil structure by forcing blocks of grout into the soil. When a number of such 'blocks' of grout are formed the intervening soil is compressed, and the ground is stiffened and strengthened in consequence.

Disturbance of near-surface soils: Grouting is rarely applied within 2m or so of the ground surface as the injection pressures are such that the ground would quickly yield and the grout would issue from the surface. However, treatment of deeper strata involves the drilling of rotary boreholes, often at very close spacings (say less than 2m), which will lead to extensive near-surface disturbance. The high pressures often used in grouting can change the structure of the soil, and so create substantial ground disturbance. Additionally waterlogging and contamination of the ground may occur as a result of grout spillages and flushing out of the grout lines after use.

The grout is generally chemically different from the ground in which it is injected, therefore if it comes into contact with archaeological remains it may cause their corrosion or decay. Indirectly the grout could affect the *in situ* preservation of remains if it alters the burial environment surrounding them, for example a cement-based and therefore alkaline grout may locally alter the 'natural' pH of the ground. This impact may be more severe within wet ground because the solution and mobilisation of salts is more likely to occur.

Mitigation of ground disturbance: To achieve minimal impact on *in situ* archaeological remains, a detailed knowledge of the soil is needed to design the grouting treatment. If permeation grouting is used, it is possible, with excellent supervision, to cause minimal ground movement because there is ideally little or no change in original soil volume and structure.

Avoidance of archaeological remains by grouting operations should be aimed for, and this will require information on the depth and likely extent of the remains before the injecting starts. Grout may then be injected via inclined boreholes, giving the scope for its injection beneath and without the need to drill through an archaeologically sensitive area.

A2.12.8 Deep drainage

Description: The insertion of 'wick' drains or sand drains vertically into a body of soil to improve its strength by the rapid relief of pore water pressures. The pore water pressure is the pressure of water in a saturated soil, such that if the pressure is zero then consolidation (improvement of strength) is complete. This process is usually allied to surcharging.

Disturbance of near-surface soils: The drains are usually inserted at close spacings (*c* 2–3m), and are usually allied to surcharging. Additionally the installation plant may require the placement of a working platform and therefore ground disturbance can be extensive.

Mitigation of ground disturbance: The spacing of drains controls the rate at which excess pore pressures are dissipated. If a slow rate of dissipation can be accommodated within the construction programme then the spacing can be increased or, in the extreme case, the drains omitted altogether. Because the removal of water from an archaeological deposit can adversely affect its *in situ* preservation, a mitigation option is the isolation of ground containing the remains from the area of deep drainage.

A2.13 Control of groundwater and drainage

A2.13.1 Introduction

Construction operations involving excavation for foundations or services may encounter groundwater at shallow depth, particularly if surface layers comprise permeable sediments. Uncontrolled groundwater pressure around a surface excavation can cause the sides of the excavation to fail or the excavation to flood. It may also cause piping of the floor of the excavation, which occurs when the seepage force associated with an upward flow of groundwater balances the downward force represented by the soil weight. Frictional resistance between the grains is reduced to zero and the condition of the deposit converts from that of a stable soil to a fluid, causing collapse of the excavation (Somerville 1988).

Where groundwater is present, specific measures must be taken to control it, the most common of which involve the exclusion or interception of groundwater. The choice of method will depend upon a variety of factors including: nature and permeability of the ground; extent of area to be dewatered; depth to the water table and extent of lowering required; and the proximity of existing structures, watercourses and water-abstraction schemes. The main techniques employed are listed in Table 2.

A2.13.2 Groundwater-exclusion methods

Description: The following methods may be used on a dewatering project:

1 Sheet piling: Steel sheets are driven into the ground. They may be a temporary or permanent measure, and can support the sides of an excavation with suitable propping.
2 Slurry trench cut-off wall: A trench is backfilled with bentonite to form a low-permeability diaphragm wall.
3 Compressed air: Used in confined chambers such as tunnels, sealed shafts and caissons. Increased air pressure balances pore water pressure in soil around the chamber, limiting ingress of water.
4 Ground freezing: Brine or liquid nitrogen is injected into the soil, forming a wall of frozen ground, which can support the side of the shaft as well as excluding groundwater.
5 Cement grouting: Grout is injected into the ground, filling pore spaces and preventing the flow of water through the soil. See Section A2.12.7.
6 Chemical and resin grouts: Grout injected into the ground by lances. Chemical grouts are used in medium sands, resins in fine sands and silts. See Section A2.12.7.
7 Jet grouting: Used for most soils and very weak rocks, typi-

Method of Control	Deposit (Granular Sediments)											
	Clay fraction	Silt fraction			Sand fraction			Gravel fraction			Boulder
		Fine	Medium	Coarse	Fine	Medium	Coarse	Fine	Medium	Coarse	
Exclusion											
Sheet piling								Ancillary pumping			
Slurry trench cut-off wall								Ancillary pumping			
Compressed air	Support only							Heavy air losses may occur			
Ground freezing											
Cement grouting	Stiff fissured clay										
Chemical and resin grouts											
Jet grouting											
Abstraction											
Gravity drainage											
Sumps											
Vertical wellpoints											
Horizontal wellpoints											
Electro-osmosis		Waterlogged soils									

Table 2   Approximate range of application of groundwater-control techniques in soils (Adapted from Somerville 1988; Blyth and de Freitas 1984)

cally forms a series of overlapping columns of soil-grout mixture. See Section A2.12.7.

Disturbance of near-surface soils: Sheet piling will cause displacement of soil, and it may require an ancillary system to cope with residual flow between elements. A slurry cut-off wall will require the excavation of a trench which may be *c* 1m wide or more, depending on the wall depth. See Section A2.12.7 for effects of grouts.

Mitigation of ground disturbance: Sheet piles and cut-off walls may be located to avoid areas of known archaeological importance. Alternatively, the remains and surrounding ground could be isolated by a containment system, in order to remove the impact of changes in the site's groundwater regime. See Section A2.12.7 for mitigation of grouting impact.

A2.13.3 Groundwater-abstraction methods

Description: The following methods may be used on a development project:

1   Gravity drainage: Suitable for low-permeability soils. On sloping sites, a gravity drain can be installed to a discharge point further downslope.
2   Sumps: A pit or sump is excavated usually in the corner of an excavation, made large enough to hold sufficient water for pumping and keep the excavation floor relatively dry. Water entering the excavation is diverted to the sump in simple trench drains.
3   Vertical wellpoints: Shallow wells comprising small well screens of about 50mm diameter and 1m or more depth. Wellpoints may be bored and fitted with individual pumps, or a series of wellpoints may be water-jetted into the soil and linked together by suction hose to a common pump. Pumping generates a drawdown of groundwater within the well, which encourages a radial flow of groundwater to the well. Typical wellpoint spacing is 0.5–3m in uniform soils, depending on the permeability of the soil and time required to obtain the necessary drawdown.
4   Horizontal wellpoints: These consist of perforated pipes laid horizontally in a trench and connected to a suitable pump. The trench may be dug by hand, suitable excavator or specialist trench-cutting machines, and backfilled after the pipe is laid.
5   Electro-osmosis: Used in waterlogged silts, soft clays and peat, causing the sediments to expel their pore water by applying an electric current through the ground between anodes and cathodes, the latter being a metal wellpoint.

Disturbance of near-surface soils: Maximum depth of sumps is generally 5–6m for surface pumps, greater if a submersible pump is installed. Rapid pumping from trench sumps may remove fines leading to failure of sides. An increase in the thickness of the unsaturated zone leads to an increase in the oxygen content of soils at depth. Consolidation of strata and ground settlement may occur as a result of the reduction in pore water pressure around a wellpoint or sump. Specialist machines for excavating trenches for horizontal wellpoints may cause unacceptable ground compaction.

Mitigation of ground disturbance: Similar mitigation options adopted for groundwater-exclusion methods may be applicable (Section A2.13.2). Archaeological consultation of the design of wellpoint systems and sumps will be important, especially if the moisture regime under which the remains are preserved is known. Unsupported sumps may be excavated with flatter sides to prevent failure in silts and sands. In very permeable formations, supporting steel sheeting may be driven deeper than the trench to lengthen the drainage path and thus reduce the flow rate. Ground settlement may be limited by a reduction in the rate of groundwater abstraction.

A3.0 Stage 3: Construction activities: foundations and earthworks

A3.1 Shallow foundations

(Bowles 1996; Tomlinson 1995)

A3.1.1 Shallow foundations: strip footings

Description: Strip footings are the simplest of foundation types and consist of a trench excavation partially filled with cast *in situ* concrete and designed to distribute the load from load-bearing walls. The concrete is usually unreinforced.

In traditional strip footings the concrete fills only the base of the trench to a minimum depth of 150mm, the supported wall is then continued upwards to ground level in brick or blockwork. This necessity to work within the trench dictates a minimum trench width of *c* 450mm. An alternative is the narrow or deep strip footing which is excavated by machine to a minimum width of 375mm, and then filled virtually to ground level with mass concrete. The depth of the footing is primarily governed by the depth to competent soil; however, minimum depths must be achieved in order to avoid foundation distortion due to seasonal ground movement and frost – these minimum depths are 1000mm in clay soils and 450mm in sandy soils (Winterkorn and Fang 1975).

Disturbance of near-surface soils: The excavated soil is, of course, completely disturbed. Disturbance of the soil adjacent to the excavation will depend upon the method of excavation and the soil strength, being greatest for the case of machine-dug trenches in soft wet soil and least for manual excavation in hard dry soils. Concrete is required and rutting beneath the wheels of the delivery vehicle may also occur. Chemical contamination of the ground due to the introduction of concrete may also impact on the buried archaeology.

Mitigation of ground disturbance: The trenches for strip footings are excavated along the route of a new development's proposed load-bearing walls. Therefore, once the site's archaeological sensitivity is known, a sympathetic building design will minimise (by avoidance) the impact of trench construction on the archaeology.

Once there is archaeological agreement on the location of strip footings, the mitigation options discussed to reduce impact from ground-investigation excavations may be applicable (see Section A1.1). For example, disturbance surrounding the area of excavation can be minimised by carrying out the works using manual methods or lightweight plant, and working when ground conditions are dry.

When forming the foundation, vehicles supplying the concrete can be located off the areas of archaeological sensitivity, and the concrete can then be supplied by either pumping or using a hopper lifted via a crane. Lining of trenches with impermeable membranes will also limit contamination of surrounding ground when the concrete is cast *in situ*.

A3.1.2 Shallow foundations: pad foundations

Description: Pad foundations are isolated units of mass or reinforced concrete supporting individual columns or small groups of columns. Pads are generally square in plan though they may be rectangular if two or more columns are to be supported, or circular if excavated by auger.

Pad foundations are cast below the zone of seasonal soil movement. When reinforcement is required in a foundation the excavated soil surface (the formation) is protected from weathering and disturbance by a 50mm blinding layer, often of lean-mix concrete, immediately after excavation. Pad footings may also be shuttered to avoid potential degradation of concrete which may occur if it is cast directly against an excavated soil face. In extremely aggressive environments, for example severely contaminated soils and groundwater, the foundation may be cast within an impermeable membrane.

Backfill around a completed pad footing is generally of compacted selected fill. The minimum size of excavation for a pad foundation is governed by the working area required to lay blinding and fix reinforcement if such is required (Winterkorn and Fang 1975).

Disturbance of near-surface soils: As strip footings.

Mitigation of ground disturbance: As strip footings.

A3.1.3 Shallow foundations: raft foundations

Description: Whereas strip and pad footings support elements of a structure (individual walls or columns) a raft may support groups of elements or the entire structure. A raft foundation is therefore a continuous slab of, generally reinforced, concrete laid on the ground. It may be either a solid slab, a beam and slab, or a cellular slab; and it is as large as, or slightly larger than, the area of the structure which it carries. By combining individual foundations into one large raft a lower bearing pressure is imposed on the soil thus enabling construction on weaker soils. In addition potential differential settlement between loaded elements, due to either foundation soil variability or uneven load distribution, is avoided (Winterkorn and Fang 1975).

Rafts may be described as rigid or flexible; this distinction is based upon the relative stiffness of the raft and the ground. A thin raft on stiff soil may be expected to deform in compliance with the ground, giving rise to modest differential vertical movements across the structure, whereas a thick raft on weak soil is unlikely to deform significantly.

The simplest raft is the slab raft. This is a lightly reinforced slab of constant thickness, cast on a layer of hard-core at or near ground level, and supporting only light loads.

When wall and column loads are substantial a thicker more heavily reinforced raft is required to distribute these loads and perhaps bridge across areas of softer soil. Rather than thickening the whole raft, this redistribution of load may be achieved more economically by thickening the raft only beneath the loaded elements.

In the case of very heavy buildings the raft is locally thickened into deep reinforced-concrete beams. These beams can either project up to ground level from a buried slab or project down from a slab near ground level.

The excavation for a raft is made either with vertical retained walls or with battered side slopes depending on space, cost and final layout.

Depending on the relative levels of the equilibrium water table and the formation, temporary dewatering measures may be required during construction and permanent drainage may be required beneath the completed slab.

Disturbance of near-surface soils: All soils within the area of the raft will be excavated, perhaps to a depth of 1m or more. Soil surrounding the excavation may be only slightly disturbed if the work is carried out from within the excavation, though this is dependent also on other site traffic, for example access for the haulage wagons needed to remove spoil. During raft construction the movement of plant may cause compaction of underlying ground. On completion, further compaction could occur due to the load imposed by the raft and any structures it supports.

Mitigation of ground disturbance: Though it is not possible to mitigate the disturbance within the excavation, disturbance of surrounding ground may be limited by adopting the options discussed for a ground investigation (Section A1.1). Load-spreading devices may be required, for example ground levels could be raised with a suitable import material and the raft constructed above. This may also avoid the need for extensive excavation of weak ground below the raft area. The selection of raft type can be important to reduce the extent or depth of ground disturbance. For example, beam and slab rafts may be more appropriate on poor soils because the beams distribute loads over the raft so that

the slab thickness can be reduced. The beams can be upstand or downstand, though the upstand is preferable because ground penetration can be minimised if the slab is founded at or close to ground level. In comparison, cellular rafts have a construction similar to reinforced-concrete basements except that the load internal walls are used to spread the load of the superstructure. They may therefore be an inappropriate foundation solution on sites requiring the *in situ* preservation of archaeological deposits.

A3.2 Deep foundations

A3.2.1 Introduction

Piles are the commonest form of deep foundation and consist of long members of concrete, steel or, rarely, timber. They act to transmit foundation loads through soil strata of low-bearing capacity to deeper soil and rock with a high-bearing capacity. This is achieved in one of two ways: if the bearing stratum is a hard and relatively impenetrable material such as rock or dense sands and clays, an 'end-bearing' or 'toe-bearing' pile can derive most of its carrying capacity from the resistance of material at its bottom end. Alternatively, if the deposits through which the piles are constructed do not themselves have much resistance then the carrying capacity of a pile is derived partly from end-bearing and partly from friction between the embedded surface of the pile and the surrounding soil. These are called 'friction piles'. There are numerous types of pile, though they all fall into one of two classes:

1 displacement piles (high or low displacement)
2 non-displacement piles

Displacement piles act to displace the soil laterally as the pile is installed; non-displacement piles are formed by the excavation of a bore in the soil which is subsequently filled with concrete. This latter type can be classified as small diameter (less than 600mm) or large diameter (greater than 600mm).

Clusters of piles may be constructed to carry heavily loaded columns. The column load is distributed between the piles by means of a pile cap which spans across the heads of all the piles in the cluster. The cap is cast below ground level and may be in the order of 0.5–2.0m thick.

Other types of deep foundations in addition to piles are deep shaft foundations and barrettes, and these are also described below (Fleming et al 1994; BS 8004: 1986).

A3.2.2 Displacement piles (driven piles)

Description: Preformed displacement piles (driven piles) comprise hollow tubes or solid section piles which are driven into the ground. They may be driven by dropping hammer, explosion, vibration or jacking, and the hollow tubes may be steel or concrete (either open toe or this may be capped as a 'closed toe').

Solid section piles may be made of concrete, steel or timber, though the latter is rarely used in the UK. Solid steel piles are of 'H'- or 'I'-shaped section and combine a high surface area with low cross-sectional area, thereby limiting ground disturbance while providing reasonable load-carrying capacity.

Cast *in situ* displacement piles are generally formed by driving a tube into the ground to form a void. The void is then filled with concrete and the tube may be left in place or withdrawn, depending on the piling system in use. A second method involves forming a void using an auger which forces the soil aside as it rotates, rather than lifting the soil to the surface (eg Atlas Piling System). The void so formed is then infilled with concrete.

In the traditional dropping-hammer system of pile driving the rig will typically comprise a skid or crawler-mounted unit with a mast to support the pile and guide the hammer. The other systems do not require a mast; the driving units in these cases are often suspended from a crane.

Disturbance of near-surface soils: The displacement caused as the piles are driven in will distort the nearby ground, and this may affect archaeological deposits unfavourably, for example: physically bending down of layers; transportation of remains into lower deposits; introduction of oxygen; and disruption of perched water tables (Biddle 1994; Dalwood et al 1994). Ground distortion may even lift the ground or other piles nearby, so involving the need to redrive those piles that were driven first. Further ground disturbance will occur if excavations are required in which to form a pile cap. This is used to tie several piles together and it is frequently constructed below ground level. The area of ground disturbance will be increased if the pile is deflected while being driven in, for example if it hits an obstruction.

The creation of ground vibration during pile driving may also impact on buried remains. Though the energy transfer to the soil during piling is poorly understood, attempts have been made to set indices as a measure of the intensity of ground vibrations. One Code of Practice from Germany sets a maximum allowable velocity of 2mm per second in soil adjacent to foundations of ruins or buildings of great historic value (Fleming et al 1994). However, because in built-up areas heavy traffic can cause velocities of $3mms^{-1}$ to be recorded 10m from a road, caution should be used when applying this Code of Practice.

Compaction of the soil by the movement of heavy plant may occur if the plant runs directly on the soil surface. Though a piling platform may avoid this, its frequent construction from demolition debris can introduce contaminated material to archaeological deposits. The mat will also impose a load to the ground surface. Though the impact of vibration during the driving in of piles is potentially more damaging to standing archaeological remains, buried *in situ* remains may also be affected (eg physical damage and movement into lower soil layers).

Mitigation of ground disturbance: The use of specialist piling contractors experienced in the use of the pile type selected by the engineer, and who are also familiar with both the ground conditions and the site's archaeological sensitivity, should be encouraged.

On archaeologically sensitive sites friction piles can be cased or 'slip coated' to reduce deformation within the archaeological deposits as they pass through.

If buried obstructions are likely to be present or ground conditions are likely to suffer unacceptable distortion during piling, bored piles with chiselling or coring facilities may be preferable to driven piles. Alternatively, preboring through any sensitive near-surface layer and the use of low displacement piles can reduce the disturbance of surrounding soils. The uncontrolled excavation and removal of buried obstructions or the overdriving of piles (causing pile deviation from the vertical) should both be avoided if excessive ground disturbance is to be prevented.

Surface rutting and compaction due to plant movements are usually minimised by the construction of a piling platform to provide a sound working surface. Sympathetic construction to minimise its impact on underlying archaeology may require the use of 'non-aggressive' materials that are laid on to a membrane system (eg a geotextile to avoid physical mixing of introduced materials into underlying ground, and a geogrid to spread load imposed by the mat and surface plant). It is also important that any such platform is constructed adequately from the outset and not introduced at a late stage in response to rapidly deteriorating working conditions.

Where a pile cap is required to tie several piles together, further ground excavation may be avoided if it is constructed above ground level. This construction above ground level can also apply to the use of ground beams linking pile caps together.

Discussions between the archaeologist and engineer may permit a variation in the pile size, spaces between piles, and also the pile layout (traditionally a grid system). Such discussions are considered important because the spatial and type variation of archaeology preserved at a site is generally more complicated than, for example, the soil/geological variation encountered by a geotechnical engineer. It is therefore suggested that, assuming the archaeological sensitivity of a site has been determined, an individual site approach is taken when designing the piling programme. This will enable the most appropriate number, spacing, size and depth of pile to be selected, and whether they be as single or grouped piles. Using this approach, the final piling solution (possibly involving a combination of pile types) should hopefully fulfil the archaeological, engineering and economical constraints imposed on the project by both the planning authority and promoter (developer). Various piling solutions are discussed by Ove Arup and Partners (Ove Arup 1991).

A3.2.3 Non-displacement piles (bored or augered piles)

Description: The simplest method of forming pile bores is the percussive or tripod method. This is similar in operation to light cable percussion boring for ground-investigation purposes. Piles formed using this method are up to 900mm diameter (though it is most often used for small-diameter piles) and depths of 30m may be achieved. The plant used is simpler and smaller than that employed on most other types of piling and therefore this technique is used where access is restricted or the budget is limited.

Tripod bored piles are bored dry where possible, any groundwater being sealed off with casing. After formation of the pile bore a reinforcing cage is installed and the pile is concreted. Casing is removed after concreting.

The majority of large-diameter piles are formed using a rotary (auger) boring method. The pile bore is formed using a lorry or crane-mounted helical or bucket auger depending on soil type. A 'lead length' of casing is installed to guide the auger. Until this is installed disturbance of the surrounding soils may be appreciable.

A second crane is in attendance to handle casing and reinforcement cages. Ideally the operation is carried out in dry conditions within a stable bore. However, if groundwater is struck or the sides of the bore show signs of collapse, it may be filled with a bentonite clay slurry to act as support and the drilling then continued through the slurry. After completion of boring the piles are reinforced and concreted.

Continuous Flight Auger (CFA) piles are a particular type of auger bored pile in which a long helical auger is drilled into the soil to full pile design depth in one operation and without removing the soil. In suitable conditions piles up to 900mm diameter can be formed using this method though less than 750mm is more common. Pile lengths are limited by the length of the auger, but depths of c 25m can be achieved. After insertion of the auger to depth, concrete is pumped down the hollow central stem while the auger is withdrawn from the ground together with the soil. The void created by the auger is thus filled immediately with concrete. After concreting has finished, a reinforcement cage may be pushed into the wet concrete using a vibrator system to force it down. This is a comparatively clean and rapid form of pile construction, requiring only the drilling rig and a concrete pump for pile formation. It is also one of the most silent methods of building a pile. However, as with all cast *in situ* piling methods, further plant is required for the removal of arisings. There has been some resistance to the technique as quality control proved rather problematic in early contracts; however, it has now gained wide acceptance.

Disturbance of near-surface soils: Soil within the pile shaft is completely disturbed. In addition, weaker soils near the ground surface surrounding the shaft may be disturbed by the drilling until temporary casing is installed. In the case of large-diameter auger bored piles the temporary casing may not be installed until the bore is already 8 or 10m deep. A potentially serious problem is the formation of cavities or overbreaks outside the nominal diameter of the pile, particularly in non-cohesive soils.

Though normally used at depth, under-reaming (belling) can increase the area of ground disturbance at the base of the pile, the void being filled with concrete during formation of the pile.

Surrounding soils may also be disturbed by the passage of the heavy plant needed to construct the piles, and by concrete delivery and spoil-removal vehicles.

The need to avoid overtoppling of heavy construction plant, as is the case for CFA and auger bored piles, usually requires construction of a piling platform or 'mat', the impact of which is discussed for displacement piles.

Mitigation of ground disturbance: As for displacement piles, though there should be less need to mitigate against the effects of vibration and ground movement down the length of the pile. Use of specialist contractors with appropriate equipment is again important to limit the ground disturbance to the cross-sectional area of the pile. For example, excessive rotation, over-rapid extraction of the auger or incorrect supply of concrete with CFA rigs by inexperienced contractors can lead to excessive soil displacement and ground contamination. When forming the borehole, mitigation options used during a ground investigation may also be relevant (see Section A1.1).

Another option to reduce disturbance of soils during the early stages of boring is the early insertion of temporary casing, particularly if there is the risk of overbreak. Use of casing may also reduce the incidence of slumping in the borehole if groundwater is encountered.

The number, diameter and depth of piles can often be adjusted for a given load situation in order to minimise disturbance to archaeological and near-surface deposits. For example, to achieve improved load capacity a broader pile can be used because it increases both friction and end-bearing capacity. However, it may be possible to use longer but smaller-diameter piles to support the same load. In some circumstances it may also be possible to reduce the overall number of piles by constructing deep piles of higher material strength. Alternatively, fewer but much larger-diameter piles could be constructed to carry the same load as a larger number of standard-sized piles.

Attention may need to be paid to under-reaming below the archaeological deposits because it can increase the bearing capacity at the pile base without an increased construction impact on the archaeology. The overall result may be a reduction in the number and/or size of piles needed for the final foundation solution, and therefore less disturbance of a site's archaeology.

A3.2.4 Minipiles or micropiles

Description: Minipiles are simply piles of small diameter, usually taken to be less than 300mm. Though usually bored, they can be of the displacement or non-displacement type and formed by any of the techniques described above. Minipiles carry a proportionally greater load per unit of cross-sectional area than larger piles; this is due to the higher material strength of individual piles (BRE 1986).

Disturbance of near-surface soils: As for displacement and non-displacement piles.

Mitigation of ground disturbance: As for displacement and non-displacement piles.

A3.2.5 Deep shaft and basement foundations

Description: Deep shaft foundations are similar to bored cast *in situ* piles; however, they are of large diameter (greater than 2m in most cases), and used, for example, in excavation for the formation of lift shafts. Larger excavations may be required if a basement is to be formed, for example a single-storey basement may require up to 4m of excavation, plus associated drainage works. The basement floor can be formed by a raft foundation, which rarely may be anchored on piles if a high groundwater is present (to control buoyancy).

Disturbance of near-surface soils: Within the excavation all archaeological remains will be lost. This is the same as for excavation during a ground investigation (Section A1.1), and for raft and piled foundations.

Mitigation of ground disturbance: Same as for excavation during a ground investigation (Section A1.1), and for raft and piled foundations. Mitigation options are limited and, if archaeological remains are to be preserved *in situ*, it may require restricting this type of foundation through the planning process.

A3.2.6 Barrettes

Description: Barrettes are individual panels of a diaphragm wall; they can act therefore as cast *in situ* concrete piles of rectangular cross-section. Cruciform or L-shaped sections can also be formed. Barrettes are capable of carrying extremely heavy loads, but are very expensive and therefore rare. In the UK large-diameter bored piles would be used in preference.

Disturbance of near-surface soils: See diaphragm wall (Section A3.3.1).

Mitigation of ground disturbance: See diaphragm wall (Section A3.3.1).

A3.3 Retaining walls and anchoring (soil nailing)

Retaining walls are built to hold back earth or other solid material. The two main forms of a retaining wall, embedded and gravity, are described below.

A3.3.1 Embedded retaining walls

Description: A wall is constructed to a depth below the final toe level of the retained slope. This relies on the strength of soil remaining in front of the wall to resist the lateral pressure from retained soil behind the wall. Such a wall acts as a cantilever and therefore must be strong in both bending and shear. Anchoring such a wall into the retained soil mass behind it, or propping it against a suitable immovable body (eg the opposite side of an excavation), reduces the cantilever action leading to economies in the wall strength and its depth of embedment.

There are four principal techniques for forming embedded retaining walls:

1   Bored pile walls: A row of bored piles will form a wall within the ground, and this may be constructed in almost any ground conditions. If the piles overlap, this impermeable structural barrier is termed a secant pile wall. If the piles are constructed close together but not touching, then it is termed a contiguous bored pile wall; this can subsequently be made impermeable by jet grouting behind the piles.

2   Diaphragm walls: Diaphragm walling describes a technique involving the excavation of rectangular panels (barrettes) within horizontal ground and backfilling these with reinforced concrete. As with bored pile walls, a line of such elements is constructed to form a structural wall below ground level. The panels are excavated using a specialised grab operated from a crane; a second crane is used to handle reinforcement cages. The grab is positioned at ground level by twin cast *in situ* concrete guide beams, usually about a metre deep, between which the ground is excavated. The excavation is infilled with a bentonite slurry during construction in order to prevent collapse of the sides.

3   Sheet pile walls: Sheet piling is a convenient technique for the rapid installation of a structural wall in the ground. Sheet piles can be composed of steel, timber or reinforced concrete. Steel is usually preferred due to its high strength, slender section and adaptability. In temporary works (where sheet piles may be readily extracted for reuse) or in marine work sheet piles have many advantages over other methods. The piles may be installed by hammer blows, by vibration, or by jacking off adjacent piles. Each method is rapid and causes little disturbance to the ground due to the low volume of soil displaced. When used in cantilever up to 3–4m height of soil can be retained; when the wall is anchored back into the retained soil then retained heights up to 20m may be possible.

The above type of retaining wall constructions are formed in essentially horizontal ground, and excavation of the soil on one side of the wall to form a basement, retained cutting, etc only occurs when the wall's installation is complete.

4   King post walls: The king post system involves the installation of upstanding piles or posts (mostly steel driven piles or steel H-sections embedded in concrete bored piles) at wide spacings, and then the fabrication of a wall, commonly of timber or precast concrete beams, between adjacent posts. Either the wall is constructed above ground and backfilled on one side to produce a retained slope, or an excavation is commenced to one side of the king posts and the wall then constructed between the posts keeping pace with the excavation as it proceeds downwards. This form of wall is usually only used in temporary works.

In the majority of cases it is uneconomical to design cantilever embedded retaining walls to retain large heights, therefore some support must be provided to the wall above excavation level. Most often this is achieved by installing props within the excavation; however, in perhaps 1 per cent of cases anchors will be drilled through the wall into the ground behind. Such anchors are commonly 10–30m long and will decline at 20–40 degrees to the horizontal (Clayton et al 1995).

Disturbance of near-surface soils: These methods are used where it is required to excavate the soil on one side of the wall to a depth of several metres, such as forming a basement. Therefore, compared to the excavation, ground disturbance from the wall construction is minimal, though it will extend below the excavation's base. Ground disturbance may be similar to that of piles (distortion of archaeological layers, introduction of oxygen, puncturing of water tables, etc).

The formation of a retaining wall uses relatively heavy plant which may lead to compaction of the soil. The driving and extraction of sheet piles are likely to cause the most disturbance to the soils behind the wall, though physically this may not be severe due to their small cross-sectional area.

Mitigation of ground disturbance: By operating plant from the side of the wall which is subsequently to be excavated the impact of compaction on the undisturbed ground can be eliminated. Within the area of excavation, loss of archaeological remains will be total. Thin walls will affect less ground than thick walls, and therefore sheet piles may be preferable to a king post system.

A3.3.2 Gravity walls

Description: The traditional gravity wall is a massive structure, with a wide base tapering up to a relatively narrow crest, that relies on its self-weight to resist the forces imposed by the retained soil. Behind such structures retained soil heights of up to 4m are common but above 6m is rare. The base width is usually a third to a half of the wall height. Such walls are made of mass concrete, stone or brick. L-shaped reinforced-concrete units perform the same purpose, often more economically. These are infilled with compacted retained soil to provide the

necessary weight required of a gravity structure, the upright of the 'L' forming the wall face.

The principle of using the weight of the soil itself to form a gravity structure is developed further in the cases of gabion walls, crib walls and reinforced-soil walls. Gabion walls are similar to traditional gravity walls but consist of flexible baskets which are infilled *in situ* with rock fragments or cobbles. The baskets are stacked up like bricks to form the traditional gravity wall geometry. Crib walls are formed from timber or reinforced-concrete elements which interlock to form a lattice. The lattice is laid on a sloping foundation and infilled with compacted granular soil, and forms, as it is raised, a backsloping wall which bears against the retained soil.

A reinforced-soil slope consists of layers of compacted soil interleaved with geotextile sheets or metal strips; facing panels are attached to the reinforcement to prevent local deterioration of the slope face. All the methods of gravity wall construction described above are built from the base of the slope upwards. They require overexcavation of the slope, at an angle which will remain stable while the wall is constructed, followed by backfilling between the excavated face and the rear face of the wall, usually with imported granular fill.

Soil nailing and anchoring may be used as support techniques in themselves; they act by strengthening a block of soil *in situ*, this then acts as a gravity wall. Excavation is carried out in front of the wall as the soil nails or anchors are installed; that is, wall construction is undertaken from the top downwards. Both types of reinforcement are installed in pre-drilled boreholes and usually consist of steel rods installed along the length of the borehole. In the case of an anchor this rod is grouted in at the 'deep' end and then tensioned from the surface. Soil nails are grouted along their full length and may be left untensioned. At the slope surface the reinforcement terminates in a groundbearing plate. The slope face is protected by either a geomembrane or a layer of sprayed concrete to prevent degradation of the surface (Clayton et al 1995).

Disturbance of near-surface soils: With the exception of soil nailing and anchoring, gravity walls are formed 'bottom-up'; that is to say, an oversteep slope is cut some way behind the position of the wall, the wall is constructed, then the void between the back of the wall and the cut slope is infilled. With this method, therefore, there is excavation of the soil on both sides of the final wall position. Impact from the physical disturbance of archaeologically sensitive ground by such excavation is therefore likely. In the case of soil-nailed or anchored walls the retained soil is perforated by the reinforcing elements; a typical spacing of these might be 1–2m horizontally and vertically. However, these decline at c 20 degrees to the horizontal and therefore may not greatly affect the near-surface soils.

Concrete gravity walls may be waterproofed on the soil side of the wall using a bitumen paint which, along with the use of imported fill and concrete, may be aggressive to the archaeology.

Mitigation of ground disturbance: The majority of ground disturbance is caused by excavation to the foundation level of the wall. Flexible walls such as gabions and crib walls will permit more differential settlement than rigid concrete walls and therefore, arguably, the founding level may be at a shallower depth for this type of wall. The lateral extent of excavation could be reduced further by the adoption of an embedded wall technique.

Following excavation it may be necessary to line the exposed soil face with a membrane, to avoid potential chemical alteration of archaeologically sensitive ground when concrete and other imported materials are placed against it.

A3.4 Underground services (manholes and sewers)

Description: Manholes are normally constructed using precast concrete chamber rings, brick, *in situ* concrete, or precast reinforced-concrete segments in shafts. Precast concrete ring manholes have the widest application, while brick manholes and *in situ* concrete manholes are more appropriate to specific locations where constraints on sewer layout or site restrictions apply. *In situ* concrete construction is more likely to be used on open sites for large chambers at relatively shallow depth (Read 1997).

Disturbance of near-surface soils: The diameter of manholes is from *c* 2m to 4.5m, although larger diameters may be necessary on very large sewers or as working shafts for the launching of tunnelling machines. Construction normally takes place within an oversized excavation area which must provide sufficient space to the outside of the structure to enable work to be undertaken externally. It may be necessary to lower the groundwater level during construction of the manholes by pumping. On completion, excavated material or imported fill material is returned around the chamber and over the roof slab before the surface is reinstated. Alternatively, shafts may be constructed as a caisson, by sinking precast concrete segments after excavation of the shaft core; construction by this method may proceed where groundwater is present.

A3.5 Earthworks

A3.5.1 Embankments

Description: Embankments are formed from locally won materials (usually from adjacent cuttings) placed in layers and compacted. In most cases the site is initially prepared by the removal of vegetation and topsoil, both of which would degrade if left in place to produce a weak layer. Soft-spots in the foundation soils are usually dug out and replaced with granular fill. A geotextile may then be placed on the formation, in order to reduce embankment settlement and to avoid mixing of the formation soils with the first fill layer which may be a coarse drainage material.

The embankment is continued upwards with side slopes being formed at a gradient which is dependent upon the strength of the material being used. The careful design of side slopes reduces the likelihood of their failure.

When constructed on soft soils, for example across alluvial plains, the embankment may be overfilled in order to increase the load on the formation soils thereby increasing the rate of settlement. After a settlement period, usually of several months (eg over winter), the embankment is cut to final profile.

Disturbance of near-surface soils: Disturbance of the soils is limited to the removal of the topsoil and vegetation and any isolated soft-spots. Compaction of the soils will occur under the embankment load. This will be accompanied, especially in soft soils, by a slight tendency for the foundation soils to spread laterally. Any embankment failure during construction is likely to disturb the foundation soils (after construction most slope failures will be shallow and will not directly affect the foundation soils).

The soil chemical and biological environment may change beneath the embankment as a result of compaction, which can reduce the soil's air content and water content. Compaction will reduce the soil permeability, which can affect local groundwater flows and so alter the water regime surrounding *in situ* archaeological remains.

Mitigation of ground disturbance: The use of geotextile laid on the formation will reduce the degree of preparation required (though vegetation and topsoil removal would still be recommended). The use of geotextile would also reduce the tendency of the formation soils to spread laterally. Compaction of weak soils may occur, though use of load-spreading geogrids may reduce this potential impact on archaeological remains. The effectiveness of a geogrid will depend on the fragility of remains, the character of ground in which they are preserved (eg compressible peat) and size of embankment.

Changes in the soil water regime may be lessened if mitigation options include the insertion of drainage underneath and surrounding the embankment. Containment of the archaeologically sensitive ground may also be necessary to mitigate against changes in soil water content.

A3.5.2 Cuttings

Description: Cuttings are formed by the excavation of soils. Usually a cutting will be formed with side slopes, their gradient being dependent upon the strength of the cut material. It is apparent that deep cuts through weak materials will result in the removal of surface soils across a wide swathe. In urban settings where land is not available to form side slopes, cuttings are often formed within retaining walls.

Disturbance of near-surface soils: Soils are removed from cuttings and therefore disturbance and loss of archaeology are total. Excavation may be by earth-scraper removing horizontal layers from the base of the cutting, or by excavator working from a vertical face. Also a site's hydrology is often affected.

Mitigation of ground disturbance: The area of disturbance can be limited by a reduction in the extent of cutting. This is a decision made early in the design process and would involve raising the overall road level, or the use of oversteep slopes and a slope-retention technique.

A4.0 Stage 4: Post-construction maintenance activities

A4.1 Underpinning of shallow foundations

Description: A technique whereby a new foundation is constructed beneath an existing foundation, or a new foundation is formed at a lower level before removal of an old foundation. Underpinning may be necessary when there is excessive movement by settlement of the existing foundations (eg from uneven load, action of tree roots, soil upheaval, etc), to permit the existing level of adjacent ground to be lowered (eg construction of a basement at a lower level) or to increase the load-bearing capacity of the existing foundations (Son and Yuen 1993).

In England the demand for underpinning has increased because of the increased incidences of foundation movement due to problematic ground conditions (eg shrinkage of clay soils), and the need to develop urban sites without requiring excessive groundworks (eg reuse of existing buildings and avoidance of unacceptable environmental damage). Though this increased demand has led to the formation of specialist underpinning contractors (eg incorporating ground injection of grout into the underpinning), the most common methods of underpinning are as follows:

1 Mass concrete: The excavation of soil beneath the existing foundation, in bays, and its replacement with mass concrete. Access pits are dug outside the building adjacent to the foundations to permit the undermining of the existing foundations. In suitable ground conditions alternate bays may be left unexcavated, forming discrete piers, otherwise all the founding soil is removed to form a continuous mass-concrete footing. The technique is generally suitable where the depth of a stable founding stratum is less than about 2m.

2 Beam and pier: A stiff reinforced-concrete beam is formed integrally with the existing foundation, this is then supported on a series of mass-concrete piers excavated and cast beneath the beam in a similar fashion to the formation of mass-concrete bays described above. The piers can be excavated to depths of *c* 4m.

3 Beam and pile: A similar method to the above beam and pier, but after construction of the beam, piles are bored down to the chosen founding stratum. This method enables the foundation loads to be transmitted to strata in excess of 4–5m deep, or for the construction of underpinning in waterlogged granular soil which is not amenable to open excavation. The piles are usually from 150mm to 400mm in diameter and are formed vertically, beneath projections in the beam.

4 Pile: Raking piles are drilled through the existing foundation and underlying soil to the chosen founding stratum. The piles are drilled from both sides of the foundation at centres of 1m or less. Minipiles are usually used, with diameters between 75mm and 150mm. Due to their slenderness, and the fact that they are inclined, the piles are usually restricted to a maximum depth of 3–4m. For similar reasons, the piles are unsuitable for use in shrinking/swelling ground (Hunt et al 1991).

Disturbance of near-surface soils: All the methods require excavation of the ground to some extent, and therefore ground will be disturbed in these excavations. However, excavations are either manual or require lightweight plant, and so peripheral disturbance is likely to be minor. Ground disturbance due to excavations is discussed in Section A1.1.

The use of grouting and piles in some underpinning methods will create similar ground disturbance to that discussed in Sections A2.12.7 and A3.2.

Mitigation of ground disturbance: It should be ascertained whether remedial underpinning is actually required on technical grounds. To some extent the techniques described above are interchangeable; the methods which require least excavation are the beam and pier and beam and pile techniques, these may therefore be preferable in reducing ground disturbance.

Mitigation options to reduce the impact from excavation, grouting and piling have previously been discussed (see Sections A1.1, A2.12.7 and A3.2).

A4.2 Roads and earthworks

Description: On roads and earthworks a variety of techniques have been developed to repair slope failures (slips). Traditionally the entire slipped mass was removed and replaced with granular material. Alternatively, the slipped soil can be strengthened (eg using geotextiles or soil nailing) or restrained (eg with gabions) before being reused (Watson 1994).

Disturbance of near-surface soils: Physical ground disturbance is likely because the repair of slope failures can involve the use of heavy equipment, mostly associated with the movement, removal and importation of soils and materials. Disturbance of the moisture regime and chemical environment within undisturbed ground may also occur with the importation of fill materials and use of grouting.

Mitigation of ground disturbance: Options for the mitigation of ground disturbance caused during excavations, access-road construction, grouting, etc have been discussed in the preceding sections. Alternatively, a carefully designed and archaeologically supervised programme of repair that confines all engineering operations to ground previously disturbed during the site's original construction may act as the most effective mitigation option.

A4.3 Services

Description: The services most likely installed during construction of a new development include water-supply pipes, manholes, drains, sewers and interceptors, and electricity and communication cables. Once installed many of these services may require maintenance or periodic repairs, and it is possible that in doing this work, ground containing archaeological remains is disturbed (WRC 1990; Read 1997).

The maintenance activities which may result in ground disturbance are as follows:

1   Cleaning: The most common methods for cleaning water pipes are simply flushing with water and air scouring. More aggressive water-pipe cleaning options require the insertion of plant into the pipe which can involve excavation down to the pipe; for example, in straight runs of simple pipe the excavation intervals for pressure scraping may be every several kilometres, drag scraping every 100–250m, abrasive pigging up to 2km, and power boring every 150m. The most used methods for cleaning sewers are jetting (high and low pressure), winching and rodding. Jetting at higher pressures of up to 2000 bar can be used for cutting tree roots. Hand excavation is generally only considered when all other methods of cleaning are not possible.

2   Lining: Once iron or steel water pipes have been cleaned they can be relined to prevent further internal deterioration. Portland cement or epoxy resin are used as non-structural lining materials, and the lining plant is installed via the excavations made for the cleaning plant. In cases where deterioration of the pipe is advanced, a variety of techniques are available for inserting a new pipe within the old metal pipe (eg slip lining, soft insertion lining, hose lining and pipe bursting). Again, plant may be installed via the excavations made for cleaning plant but further excavations are required at each junction or valve.

   Sewer renovation with liners includes the installation of steel mesh 'planks' to form a lining, which is then injected with cement mortar to form a smooth surface. An *in situ* lining may be formed by pumping the lining material, generally concrete, between steel formwork panels. Grouts may be injected between the lining and the existing sewer, termed 'annulus grouting', and into voids external to the existing sewer, termed 'void grouting'.

3   Localised repair: Individual defects in sewers are now commonly repaired using localised no-dig techniques, for example internal patching systems using glass fibre or epoxy resin impregnation.

4   New pipe laying: New pipe may be relaid in conventionally excavated trenches, 'narrow' trenches dug by chain trenchers and mole ploughs, or using trenchless methods. Trenchless methods involve the microtunnelling techniques of moling or fluid jet cutting (high-pressure water and air jets). For these methods the only surface excavations are the launch and reception pits for the plant.

Disturbance of near-surface soils: Maintenance or repair can involve excavation to gain access to the buried pipe or cable. If conducted within previously disturbed ground (eg granular fill of originally excavated trench), the resulting excavation is unlikely to impact on archaeologically sensitive deposits. However, this can be problematic on some old sewers and pipes that were constructed by tunnelling, and therefore can have undisturbed archaeological deposits overlying them.

If water from the use of high-pressure jets is able to penetrate ground surrounding a buried pipe, localised washing out of archaeological material may occur. Penetration into surrounding ground by grout and other lining materials used in sewer repair can cause physical disruption and chemical alteration of archaeologically sensitive ground.

Mitigation of ground disturbance: Containment of excavations within previously disturbed ground, and the provision of a watching brief, may be the most effective mitigation options. Ideally the original trenches will have been backfilled with gravel or some other foreign material, which will be highly visible during re-excavation and so should minimise the risk of overdigging into undisturbed deposits.

Archaeological mitigation options could include the incorporation of existing stringent working practices that have been designed to cause minimal disruption to surface activities (road usage, public access and business operations) during service repairs or maintenance. Though not developed with archaeological *in situ* preservation in mind, these practices include trenchless replacement of pipes, use of closed-circuit television (CCTV) to locate faults, and remotely controlled repairs over long distances to avoid excavation of regular access points to the pipe.

APPENDIX B: PLANNING FRAMEWORK AND OPERATIONAL METHODOLOGIES IN ENGLAND

B1.0 Introduction to the planning framework

Section 57 of the Town and Country Planning Act 1990 states that planning permission is required for development. A development is defined as 'the carrying out of building, engineering, or mining or other operations in, on, over or under land, or the making of any material change in the use of any building or other land'.

The control of development or planning control in England and Wales is administered centrally through the Office of the Deputy Prime Minister. Detailed administration is carried out by Local Planning Authorities (LPA). In the Shire counties (ie non-metropolitan counties) there is a two-tier system of Local Planning Authority: the county council (or LPA) is responsible for the development of a broad planning policy, while the district council (DPA) has responsibility for routine planning control. The six metropolitan counties and Greater London have a single-tier Local Planning Authority represented by the metropolitan district and London borough councils and the City of London Corporation.

The principal legislation relating to planning control is the Town and Country Planning Act 1990, supplemented by the Planning (Listed Buildings and Conservation Areas) Act 1990, the Planning (Hazardous Substances) Act 1990, the Planning (Consequential Provisions) Act 1990, and the Planning and Compensation Act 1991. Under this legislation, the planning authorities are obliged to maintain Development Plans which are constantly updated and act as the basis for planning decisions. The structure of the Development Plan follows that of the LPA, ie the shire counties operate two-tier Development Plans. A unitary Development Plan is operated by the metropolitan counties and Greater London. At county level a Structure Plan is developed, in which the general policies in respect of the development and use of land are stated. The DPA is responsible for the Local Plan, which provides detail for the area covered by the Structure Plan.

In addition to the Development Plan, the Local Planning Authority may produce supplementary planning guidance which can refer in detail to a particular site or to a particular type of development.

Planning work at all levels is facilitated by Development Control Policy Notes and Planning Policy Guidance Notes issued by the Office of the Deputy Prime Minister. These concentrate on practical matters of policy formation, and will influence the contents of Development Plans. The legal effect of Development Plans is indirect insofar as their main function is guidance in the formation of policy; it is in the breach of that policy that legal constraints may apply.

B2.0 Planning permission and its relationship to archaeology

English Heritage (statutorily known as the Historic Buildings and Monuments Commission for England, or HBMC(E)), formed in 1984, is the statutory adviser to Government, planning authorities and developers on archaeological matters.

Archaeological remains are not mentioned *per se* within the main planning legislation, however Planning Policy Guidance Note (PPG) 16 *Archaeology and planning* (1990) states that 'detailed development plans [ie local plans and unitary development plans] should include policies for the protection, enhancement and preservation of sites of archaeological interest and of their settings'. English Heritage has produced further guidance in this regard (English Heritage 1992). The presence of archaeological remains therefore becomes 'a material consideration in determining planning applications'.

In addition, certain developments may also require an environmental statement to be prepared and accepted before planning permission can be considered. The contents of such an environmental statement must include the likely impact of the proposed development on 'cultural heritage' (Town and Country Planning (Assessment of Environmental Effects) Regulations 1988). The Institute of Field Archaeologists' *Standard and guidance* notes (see below) also outline the purposes and requirements of archaeological works necessary during the course of development, as instructed by the Planning Authority. In brief, they aim to examine the archaeological resource to inform on its date, character, extent, state of preservation and relative quality, to enable either:

1 The formulation of strategies for its preservation *in situ* or the management of the remains

2 The formulation of mitigation strategies to planning applications which may affect the archaeological remains, or

3 The formulation of proposals and, where necessary, excavation strategies to further define or make a lasting record of the resource prior to its loss through the site's development.

Certain classes of development are granted automatic planning permission under the terms of Development Orders issued by the Office of the Deputy Prime Minister. These Development Orders are contained in the Town and Country Planning General Development Order 1988 (GDO) and its amendments. The Permitted Developments given in the GDO include works at one location of less than 28 days' duration in any one year which do not result in material change to the land, and works carried out by highway authorities and other statutory undertakers relating to maintenance or the provision of a service. Furthermore, planning control does not apply to Crown land including that held in trust by government bodies. However, in the cases of statutory undertakers and Crown land, informal consultation procedures exist which have a similar effect to standard planning control procedures.

Additionally, planning legislation is relaxed in areas designated as Enterprise Zones or Simplified Planning Zones.

B3.0 Legislation

Four groups of legislation issued by Parliament relate to archaeology:

1 Protection of ancient monuments.
2 Town and country planning.
3 Countryside legislation.
4 Operation process of energy and utility processes.

Statutory protection is afforded under the Ancient Monuments and Archaeological Areas of Interest Act 1979 to monuments of national importance which have been scheduled under that Act (Breeze 1993). As preservation *in situ* is now the preferred strategy for ensuring the preservation of archaeological remains, no new AAIs have been added to the original list of five (York, Chester, Hereford, Exeter and Canterbury).

The statutes containing implications for archaeological consideration in development projects are described by McGill, and Pugh-Smith and Samuels, and they are listed below (cf McGill 1995, 99, table 5.2; Pugh-Smith and Samuels 1996):

Agriculture Act 1986
Ancient Monuments and Archaeological Areas Act 1979
Burial Act 1857
Care of Cathedrals Measure 1990
Coal Industry Nationalisation Act 1946
Coal Industry Act 1990
Coal Mining Subsidence Act 1991
Coastal Protection Act 1949
Countryside Act 1968
Disused Burial Grounds Act 1884 and 1981
Electricity Act 1989
Forestry Act 1967
Highways (Assessment of Environmental Effects) Regulations 1988
Land Drainage Act 1976 and 1991
National Heritage Act 1983
Opencast Coal Act 1958
Planning and Compensation Act 1991
Planning (Listed Buildings and Conservation Areas) Act 1990
Protection of Wrecks Act 1973
Town and Country Planning Act 1990
Transport and Works Act 1992
Water Act 1989
Water Resources Act 1991
Wildlife and Countryside Act 1981

Internationally, the treatment of human remains is covered in a guidance document: the Vermillion Accord (World Archaeological Congress 1987) and the International Council on Museums 1986 Code of Ethics (Parker-Pearson 1995).

The European Convention on the Protection of the Archaeological Heritage, or Valletta Convention, approved in 1992 by the Council for Europe, covers issues including the maintenance of archaeological inventories for each country; designation of protected status for new archaeological sites or areas; metal detection; development impact assessment; and trade in antiquities (McGill 1995; Darvill 1996).

B4.0 Regulations for contract archaeologists

The Institute of Field Archaeologists is the professional body to which many archaeologists actively engaged in field archaeology are aligned. It has established standards and guidance notes for the practice and conduct of British archaeologists, which have been generally accepted across the board for the execution of archaeological work. These principles form the basis for the curatorial monitoring of work conducted for both development and research purposes. If negligent or unethical work is in evidence, disciplinary procedures may follow an investigation conducted by the IFA Disciplinary Committee.

For further information on the codes of conduct, standards and guidance notes, refer to:

Institute of Field Archaeologists: By-Laws of the Institute of Field Archaeologists: *Code of conduct,* revised 2000

Institute of Field Archaeologists: By-Laws of the Institute of Field Archaeologists: *Code of approved practice for the regulation of contractual arrangements in field archaeology,* revised 2000

Institute of Field Archaeologists: *Standard and guidance for archaeological desk-based assessment,* revised 2001

Institute of Field Archaeologists: *Standard and guidance for archaeological field evaluation,* revised 2001

Institute of Field Archaeologists: *Standard and guidance for an archaeological watching brief,* revised 2001

Institute of Field Archaeologists: *Standard and guidance for archaeological excavation,* revised 2001

APPENDIX C: CASE STUDY OF BLUE BRIDGE LANE, YORK

C1.0 Introduction

This case study documents the route pursued from the conception of a development through design and pre-construction groundworks to the creation of a mitigation strategy for a site in York (Evans 1994; Griffiths 1995). The case study illustrates the involvement that various archaeological and engineering professionals had in a developer-led project that aimed to economically develop a site in an archaeologically acceptable manner.

The development site was bounded to the east by Fishergate Road, to the west by the riverbank at the confluence of the Rivers Ouse and Fosse, to the north by modern offices and other buildings, and to the south by Fishergate House – a Grade II Listed building (Figure 28).

C2.0 History of the development

In 1993 a planning application was submitted to York City Council to build a development of two-, three- and four-storeyed sheltered/retirement housing in Fishergate, York. The development, at Blue Bridge Lane in the south of the city, is located within the Area of Archaeological Importance (as designated in the 1979 Act). The underlying solid geology consists of Bunter Sandstone overlain by drift geology of Glacial Tills and warped lacustrine clays capped by alluvium. A pile and raft foundation strategy was proposed in order to preserve as much as possible of the known archaeology *in situ*, using the least archaeologically intrusive method. Pre-construction works began in November 1993 and planning permission was granted in April 1995. At the time of writing, the development had not yet proceeded to the construction phase and some aspects had been removed or changed (a revised scheme was then approved by York City Council which would require further archaeological evaluation); notwithstanding this, the site is an excellent example of the processes entailed in developing an archaeological mitigation strategy.

C3.0 Personnel involved with the development

1 Developer
2 Consultant Archaeologist
3 Local Government Curator
4 Archaeological Contractor
5 Architect
6 Consulting Engineers

C4.0 Archaeological evidence

Documentary evidence, an archaeological evaluation and previous archaeological work in the vicinity of the development area indicated that considerable and significant archaeology would be found on the site. Archaeological remains included Roman cremations (*c* 1st–2nd centuries AD), an Anglian trading centre or *wic*, a Gilbertine priory, and post-medieval and modern dumps.

A series of eight trenches were archaeologically excavated in two consecutive phases of investigation (Figure 28). Trenches A and C were machine excavated to the natural, the remainder hand excavated after the modern concrete or tarmac was removed. Two of the geotechnical boreholes were subject to an archaeological watching brief and samples were taken of the deposits for analysis. Trenches A, B and C were 3m x 3m in size and D, E, F, G and H were originally 2m x 2m, reduced to 1m x 1m at the archaeological levels.

Trenches A, B, C and H were located on a north–south ridge which extends parallel to the River Ouse. The land surface slopes gradually eastwards to Fishergate and more markedly towards the Ouse to the west. Trench G was the most westerly trench and showed the greatest depth of overburden above the archaeology (Table 3). The slope of the natural surface towards the river ensured excellent drainage of the deposits as a result of the dryness of the soil. Environmental evidence suggested that the preservation of biological remains would be poor across the site, particularly for material preserved in anaerobic, waterlogged conditions (Evans 1994).

Overall, the archaeological investigations did not identify any features that positively dated to the Roman period, but residual artefacts did suggest that there was some activity in the area. The Anglian period (5th–9th centuries) was represented by a possible post and beam structure and an ambiguously dated burial. The medieval period was represented in almost all the trenches and showed agricultural or horticultural activity as well as a cobbled surface – probably indicating the location of a medieval road junction. The post-medieval and modern periods were characterised by episodes of dumping across the site.

Based on the results of the evaluation, the developer and consultant archaeologist presented a mitigation strategy which took into account the varied archaeological evidence expected within the bounds of the development.

C5.0 Mitigation strategy

The mitigation strategy for Blue Bridge Lane exists as a concise stand-alone document including detailed drawings of the specifications describing exactly which foundations would be utilised in specified locations across the site. It was not an unexpected document born of contingency, but rather one which was foreseen and planned for from the conception of the development. It was devised by the consultant archaeologist in consultation with the developer, the engineers and the architect, thus ensuring that all needs were met and, most importantly, that the archaeology would be subjected to the least construction impact possible. The document covers pre-site preparation, construction and post-construction activities. Definitions of standard terms and diagrams of the foundation types are given so that the method is easily understood by all, and not simply by the

Figure 28 Plan of Blue Bridge Lane site showing locations of test trenches (A–H), boreholes (BH1–BH8) and areas of archaeological mitigation (1–11) (not to scale)

Trench	Ground surface (height in m OD)	Minimum height of archaeology	Maximum height of archaeology	Height of significant archaeology
A	14.17m	0.65m	1.10m	0.65m
B	14.20m	0.80m	1.10m	0.95m
C	14.20m	0.10m	0.75m	0.30m
D	12.90m	No archaeology	—	—
E	12.05m	0.26m	1.45m	0.26m
F	11.80m	0.20m	1.60m	0.40m–0.80m
G	11.15m	1.10m	1.80m	1.10m
H	14.25m	0.50m	0.80m	0.50m–0.80m

Table 3 Depths of archaeological strata across Blue Bridge Lane

technical experts. The schedule of meetings and site operations undertaken between November 1993 and August 1997 which resulted in the documented mitigation strategy for the site are summarised in Table 4.

It is important to note that preservation by record was an option discussed in the preliminary planning stages but was discounted on the projected costs. A similar site in Fishergate had been excavated in the late 1980s at a cost of approximately £900,000; similar projected costs were deemed unfeasible by the Blue Bridge Lane developer and thought likely to jeopardise the financial viability of the development. The mitigation strategy as highlighted below had not been implemented at the time of writing; when construction does proceed the site may be reduced in area.

The approved mitigation strategy was developed using a zonal approach in which the site was zoned into a total of 11 different areas. The mitigation strategy as it applied to the different areas is summarised below.

Areas 1 and 1A

No archaeological evaluation done in this area – assumption made that there would be significant archaeological deposits here. A combined foundation design proposed utilising two sets of parallel shallow piles at 90 degrees to Fishergate supporting a precast or cast *in situ* concrete raft. Its base to be no less than 550m from the FFL (Finished Floor Levels). Maximum pile diameter of 400mm.

Area 2

Traditional strip foundations used here as previous ground reduction in medieval/post-medieval period removed most archaeological deposits. Watching brief to be conducted during trenching.

Area 3

Natural ground surface slopes down towards river in this area. Use of semi-shallow piles combined with an FFL of 13.30m.

Construction depth of 900mm will allow pile to be contained within late deposits.

Area 4

Construction of lift shaft and bridge access necessitates total archaeological excavation and recording.

Area 5

The FFL in this area will allow use of standard piles and ground beams with a construction depth of 1300mm.

Area 5A

Medieval staithe (landing stage) located in this area. Shallow piles will be placed parallel to the postulated line of the quay and should straddle it. The line will be probed by hand auger prior to construction. If the quay is found to lie in the direct path of the piles, the layout will be redesigned to ensure the preservation of the feature *in situ*.

Area 5B

Considerable depth of modern made ground in this area means that standard piles can be used and are not likely to impact on the archaeology.

Area 5C

This area will have a lower external wall on the finished building which needs to be supported by foundations placed on the current ground level. These will be stepped along the Blue Bridge Lane side allowing for the slope down to the west. The whole foundation will be piled and supported on a ground beam. The combined depth will be restricted wherever possible to the modern deposits. A watching brief will be necessary.

Date	Event	Method	Location
11/93–07/94	Project conception and pre-construction groundworks	Planning restrictions and archaeological potential of site noted; engineering works discussed with consultant archaeologist. Discussions with City Council Archaeologist regarding aims of evaluation. AAI permissions granted.	
08/94	Phase 1 investigations	Phase 1 of the archaeological evaluation completed (Trenches A, B, C, D, F). Engineering boreholes (BH1–7) dug in conjunction with the archaeological works. Two test trenches backfilled using Type 1 and sand capped by tarmac.	Areas 1A; 2; 3; 5B; courtyard of 6; 7; 8
09/94	Results of evaluation surveys	Option to preserve archaeology *in situ* adopted. Further works needed for both archaeological and engineering data.	
10/94	Phase 2 investigations	One additional borehole (BH8) and three testpits excavated (Trenches E, G, H).	Area 3; courtyard of 5; 7
11/94–02/95	Drafting of mitigation strategy	In-house discussions re: mitigation; revisions to building plans; foundation strategy and Finished Floor Levels (FFL) of 13.30m and 13.55m agreed; mitigation proposals discussed with City archaeologist.	
03/95	Mitigation strategy approved	City archaeologist approves Mitigation Document.	All areas
04/95–11/96	Site preparation	Planning permission granted; final technical drawings produced. Upstanding 1960s' office building demolished with concomitant archaeological watching brief.	All areas
08/97		Housing development not yet implemented.	

Table 4 Schedule of events leading to the mitigation strategy

Areas 6 and 8

Probable location of Anglian inhumation cemetery necessitates careful mitigation. Shallow piles will be used in both areas, impacting only on the upper, modern deposits. Specified places in both areas will be subject to ground raising in order to restrict the pile caps and ground beams to the modern levels.

Area 7

The access road in this area will impact on a 6m x 10m corri-dor through the Anglian cemetery. Full archaeological excavation will be done here.

Area 9

Considerable depth of modern made ground in this area means that standard piles used for the bridge abutment should not impact upon the archaeology.

Area 10

World War II bunker in this area will be recorded and

photographed prior to the substructure being backfilled with the roof and other above-ground materials. The building will be left *in situ* for future archaeologists.

Area 11

Post-construction landscaping activities around Fishergate House will be restricted to areas of known recent dumped material. The trees and shrubs will be shallow-rooting varieties so their roots do not impact upon the archaeology. Service locations will be finalised with the appropriate agencies and all efforts will be taken to safeguard and record archaeological deposits when and wherever possible.

C6.0 Comments and discussion

Although this mitigation strategy had not yet been implemented at the time of writing, it is an excellent example of how to plan and achieve preservation *in situ* within the context of developer-led archaeology. The archaeologically aware developer commissioned the services of an archaeological consultant at the earliest possible stage in the development's planning process, thus enabling the developer to plan for any effects that the construction might have on the archaeology – be they engineering, landscaping or architectural-related design problems. This is absolutely crucial in ensuring that the archaeology on a site is dealt with constructively and comprehensively within the limits of the specific development. The strategy outlined above is useful in showing the route the mitigation process can take when it is an option envisaged from the outset of a development. The production of a stand-alone mitigation strategy document is unusual and should be encouraged for future developments: not only as a tool for the developer/client but also for the curator and consultant/contracting archaeologists. It is a useful mechanism for clearly stating exactly what construction processes will take place where on a development site and how they will be mitigated to restrict their impacts on the underlying archaeology.

APPENDIX D: LITERATURE REVIEW AND BIBLIOGRAPHY

D1.0 Introduction

The following document is a bibliographic listing of articles related to the subject of archaeological preservation *in situ*. The document has been subdivided into four sections:

1 UK archaeological references – annotated examples of mitigation strategies in the UK.
2 International archaeological references – annotated examples of international mitigation strategies, predominantly in North America.
3 Mitigation/preservation *in situ* theory and trends – background theory and trends in both the UK and North America.
4 Technical and scientific research – research into techniques of preservation *in situ*, and related fields, carried out in the UK and internationally. This section is subdivided into three parts: work of the US Army Corps of Engineers and other US Federal departments; UK technical and scientific work; and other work which may be indirectly relevant (UK and international).

Every effort has been made to ensure that the bibliography is comprehensive in its coverage of the subjects of preservation *in situ* and the mitigation of construction impacts, and it is hoped that this will allow the document to be used as a versatile starting point for those wishing to find out more about this subject area. The dominance of North American references throughout the document is not due to any overt bias of the authors, but a reflection of the fact that American archaeology has been concerned in print with this subject for a longer period than has been the case in the UK. British archaeology has only recently begun to really address the issues in print, and research the effectiveness of the methods and strategies involved in implementing the practice of preservation *in situ*.

Further references may also be found on the world wide web at a site maintained by the University of Arkansas. The National Archaeological Database is specifically for US examples, but contains much of interest for research in the UK. Its address is: www.cast.uark.edu/products/NADB/. The reference lists can be searched using key words. In a different format, the Council for British Archaeology's *Britarch* server provides a somewhat similar function.

D1.1 Acknowledgements

This document was compiled from the following sources: University of Cambridge Libraries; the British Library; the Internet; I Oxley, St Andrews University; P Hinton, MoLAS; project team members S Cole, English Heritage, and M Davis, Hunting Technical Services; and from bibliographies of references cited below.

D2.0 UK archaeological examples

Ashurst, J, Balaam, N and Foley, K, 1989 The Rose Theatre: overcoming the technical preservation problems, *Conservation Bulletin* 9, 9–10
One of a very few examples in the UK where the mitigation strategy has been published. The authors give a relatively detailed outline of the reasons for preserving the archaeological remains of the Rose Theatre, London. They clearly state the materials used and why, as well as how the scheme was implemented. The strategy was designed to be controllable and to be as neutral as possible in terms of soil pH. The article concedes that while the site is preserved in the short term, there are still issues to be discussed in the long term regarding the re-excavation of the site and its presentation to the public.

Barber, B, 2002 'Saving the Globe?': part 2: The preservation of the monument, *London Archaeologist* 9 (12), 323–9
This paper describes the scheme for protecting the Globe Theatre remains *in situ* by the archaeologist responsible for implementing the preservation scheme. Although ambivalent about the solution that was adopted, Barber comments that the complex methodological problems that were raised have not yet been resolved.

Biddle, M, 1989 The Rose reviewed: a comedy (?) of errors, *Antiquity* 63, 753–60
Commentary on the contentious case of the Rose Theatre from a third-party point of view. The paper highlights six main problems, one of which was the time delay in deciding how to

preserve the site. This resulted in decisions being made in a relatively short period which perhaps were not in the best interest of the site, especially in relation to its preservation and future display. Both designs for the display hall are briefly presented, giving the reader some idea of how preservation and presentation to the public of similar remains could be achieved.

Catherall, P D, 1980 Archaeology and gas pipelines, *Gas Engineering and Management* 20, 471–6

Although an old reference, this paper tackles the archaeological problems faced by large pipeline works, and gives examples of mitigation by avoidance. Probably more useful for the non-archaeologist, eg engineers, developers, the utility companies, etc.

Corfield, M, Hinton, P, Nixon, T and Pollard, M (eds), 1998 *Preserving archaeological remains* in situ: *proceedings of the conference of 1st to 3rd April 1996,* Museum of London and University of Bradford, London

Proceedings of the 1996 conference held in London. This attracted a wide range of professionals from archaeologists, engineers, environmentalists, architects, etc who are involved in decisions to preserve and monitor archaeology *in situ.* Papers covered the burial environment on land and the intertidal/ marine zone (physical, chemical, biology and groundwater regimes), available mitigation strategies and approaches to site monitoring, and the planning framework as it applies to preservation *in situ.* (The *Proceedings* of the 2nd conference held 12th to 14th September 2001 are in preparation.)

Dalwood, C H, Buteux, V A and Darlington, J, 1994 Excavations at Farrier Street and other sites north of the city wall, Worcester 1988–1992, *Transactions of the Worcestershire Archaeological Society* 3 (14), 75–114

Extensive, nationally important Roman deposits were discovered during archaeological field evaluation on this site in Worcester. A modification in the development's design enabled the Roman features to be preserved *in situ.* This paper is instructive in noting the distortion caused by driven piles on this particular site, especially their effect on artefacts and stratigraphy. The authors note that the disturbance caused by the piles was greater than they had at first expected.

Darvill, T and Gerrard, C, 1994 *Cirencester: town and landscape: an urban archaeological assessment,* Cotswold Archaeological Trust, Cirencester

Although primarily concerned with the archaeology of Cirencester, 'Part IV: Archaeology and development' contains pertinent information. The authors clearly explain the various legal frameworks which affect archaeology in general, and highlight the archaeological process from appraisal through to the implementation of an archaeological strategy. The process is discussed in detail to show how archaeology and development can be integrated from the earliest possible moment to prevent

delays and subsequent extra costs. The most common foundations types are discussed under the *management options* section. Piles are discussed at length, and the results of the 1991 Ove Arup study in York (see below) are referred to in terms of spacing and pile size.

Drummond-Murray, J, 1994 Wolseley Street, land adjacent to the Fire Station, SE1, London Borough of Southwark: an archaeological evaluation, Museum of London Archaeology Service report, London

This report includes details of a backfilling regime used as the mitigation strategy to preserve a site of prehistoric ard marks. The site was significant as it was only the second of its type to be found in the London area. The mitigation strategy had three distinct aims identified prior to implementing a strategy comprised of Terram, sharp grade 60 salt and lime-free sand, and a capping of spoil.

Hunting Technical Services, 1996 Archaeological deposit monitoring at 44/45 Parliament Street, York: report detailing the installation of monitoring points: report R1052, Hunting Technical Services, Hemel Hempstead

Following an archaeological evaluation by York Archaeological Trust, a programme of deposit monitoring was established at a redevelopment site in York. Monitoring of the moisture levels and quality of water within the *in situ* archaeological deposits was undertaken at regular intervals using a range of devices. The monitoring data are reported for a period before construction, then during and finally after construction of the new Marks and Spencer store.

Hunting Technical Services, 1997 Installation of preservation backfill at Anchor Terrace car park, 1–15 Southwark Bridge Road, London SE1: report R1162, Hunting Technical Services, Hemel Hempstead

Report detailing all aspects of a mitigation strategy used to achieve preservation *in situ* of a site containing remains associated with the Globe Theatre, a Scheduled Ancient Monument. The area to be covered by the preservation backfill had previously been covered by a number of temporary preservation strategies installed following the site's archaeological evaluation in 1989. These temporary strategies had been monitored on a monthly basis and details of the monitoring programme are included in this report. The site's preparation by staff from the Museum of London and then the installation of a silica sand and builder's sand backfill under a waterproof membrane system are described.

Hunting Technical Services, 1997 Interim report to Barratt London detailing archaeological deposit monitoring at Bishop's Depository, 1–12 Belgrave Road, London: report R1158, Hunting Technical Services, Hemel Hempstead

Report of the first stage of a monitoring project looking at possible changes in archaeologically important alluvial deposits located on a site proposed for redevelopment. Work undertaken to recover and characterise the deposits is described, and the monitoring rational is summarised.

Klemperer, W and Stillitoe, P, 1995 James Brindley at Turnhurst Hall: an archaeological and historical investigation, *Staffordshire Archaeological Studies* 6
An example of a published mitigation strategy and partial excavation of an 18th-century canal garden feature in the grounds of Turnhurst Hall prior to development. The mitigation strategy utilised a combination of excavation, backfilling, and a raise and raft foundation over the possible canal. The authors believe that the methods used in this instance achieved the long-term preservation *in situ* of the reputed model lock designed by James Brindley while he lived at the house.

Neal, V, 1992 Appendix A, in 82–86 Park Lane, Croydon, Surrey: report on archaeological evaluations (R Nielson), Museum of London Archaeology Service report, London
Report on the strategy used to backfill the area of the graves and pits recorded on the site at Park Lane. A system combining Terram, damp soil and damp fine-grade sharp sand was used over the features. The whole site was then covered in three overlapping layers of Terram, 6 inches of sand and capped with spoil, taking care to ensure that air was exluded from the edges of the backfilled area.

Neal, V, 1993 Appendix H, in Deen City Farm Grazing, Varley Way, Mitcham, London Borough of Merton: an archaeological evaluation (R Nielson), Museum of London Archaeology Service report, London
A temporary backfilling regime used to preserve burials *in situ* is described in an appendix to the main evaluation report. A layer of Terram 1500 was placed over the graves and covered by a 100mm layer of sharp grade 60 salt and lime-free sand. The area was capped by spoil. Brass and galvanised steel fittings were included in the backfill as an innovative means of deterring metal detectors.

O'Sullivan, H, 1996 82–90 Park Lane, Croydon: a planning case-study, *London Archaeologist* 7 (16), 424–31
This paper deals with the 1995 planning appeal of a site in Croydon, London. The views expressed are those of an observer of the process, but nonetheless are of interest here as they highlight the fact that the desire to preserve *in situ* is not always the most preferred option of archaeologists. The area to be developed incorporates an Anglo-Saxon cemetery of national importance which the developer, on advice from English Heritage, agreed to preserve *in situ*. The paper discusses the contentious mitigation issues and the appeal which resulted in the final outcome of preservation *in situ*. The paper suggests that PPG 16 fails to take account of the circumstances of the archaeology in question and its academic or research potential; in effect, that it is being applied wholesale without regard to the practicalities (see also Welch 1997 below).

Ove Arup & Partners and the Department of Archaeology, University of York in association with B Thorpe, 1991 *York development and archaeology*, Manchester
This study is a useful tool for understanding the symbiotic relationships that exist between archaeology and engineering techniques. Ove Arup were commissioned by York City Council to examine the situation between archaeology and development in York, and to 'provide a framework for ensuring the development of sites is secured in a way which can conserve the most outstanding archaeological resources' (p1). Ove Arup concluded that the underlying geological strata in York dictate the use of piling as the main foundation design. The study outlines the potential effects piled foundations may have, both beneficially and detrimentally, to the archaeological deposits in York. While the report deals exclusively with York and its particularities, it may be seen as a guide for how to mitigate construction impacts, especially for engineers and architects seeking ways to contain the impact of their developments/foundation designs. Having been produced expressly for York's archaeology and its particular urban environment, it is only useful as a rule of thumb when used for comparative purposes in other locations.

Ove Arup & Partners, 1997 The Governor's House: an engineering and archaeological strategy: internal report, Ove Arup & Partners, London
Description of the engineering techniques used on a site in London where preservation *in situ* was achieved by mitigating the construction impacts. Effective and well-designed case study with information of interest to developers, engineers and archaeologists.

Pryor, F, 1991 *Flag Fen: prehistoric Fenland centre*, English Heritage, London

Pryor, F, 1992 Current research at Flag Fen, Peterborough, *Antiquity* 66 (251), 439–57
These two references together describe the methods used to preserve part of the post alignment and platform at Flag Fen, Peterborough – one of the few published preservation *in situ* mitigation schemes. The former outlines the methods used to construct the artificial mere (1991, 24) while the latter deals with the construction of a raft to float the visitors' centre over the archaeology under the mere (1992, 442–3). Although Flag Fen was not initially threatened by construction activities but by rapid dewatering, this example is useful for showing how preservation of waterlogged deposits can be achieved. The second reference sets out the mitigation strategy designed for the construction of a building over the preserved waterlogged deposits.

Reynolds, P, 1996 Pile system cuts heritage costs, *Contract Journal* 344, 21
Brief summary of a pile-extraction system used by Bachy that enables replacement of redundant piles with new piles. Reference

is made to the Governor's House project in central London where 19 old piles were removed and replaced with 26 new piles without significant disturbance to the buried Roman site.

Rowsome, P, 1996 The Billingsgate Roman house and bath: conservation and assessment, *London Archaeologist* 7 (16), 415–23
Although this article is primarily concerned with describing the excavation history and the present conservation issues of the bath-house, it does briefly describe the original measures taken to preserve the site *in situ* beneath a 1970s' office block. The present conservation work is a result of incorrect materials originally used to consolidate and cap the site.

Sanderson, I, 1996 Old Hall Farm, Pontefract: reburial of the partially excavated masonry remains: revised brief to ensure the preservation of the archaeological value of the site: unpublished archaeological brief prepared by West Yorkshire Archaeology Service
This details the proposed and subsequently utilised scheme of reburial used to preserve *in situ* masonry foundations beneath open space. The scheme used a combination of geotextile fabric and Hensall sand capped by topsoil with short grasses and wild flowers with minimal root disturbance.

Wainwright, G J, 1989 Saving the Rose, *Antiquity* 63, 430–5
Description of the process leading up to, and the methods taken for, the preservation of the Rose Theatre remains discovered in London in 1988–9. The preservation method was designed to enable the future excavation, conservation and presentation of the site to the public. The author stresses that the steps taken to preserve the remains *in situ* can only be seen as a short-term measure of preservation as the long-term maintenance and preservation problems are unknown (see also Ashurst et al 1989 above).

Welch, M, 1997 The Anglo-Saxon cemetery at 82–90 Park Lane, Croydon, Surrey: excavation or preservation? *London Archaeologist* 8 (4), 94–7
A short article expressing doubts regarding the use of preservation by burial in order to preserve the Anglo-Saxon cemetery *in situ*. The author favoured full excavation in this case, and presents his argument against preservation *in situ*.

D3.0 International archaeological examples

Ardito, A J, 1994 Reducing the effects of heavy equipment compaction through *in situ* archaeological site preservation, *Antiquity* 68, 816–20
A short article on an example of an experiment in temporary preservation *in situ* through site burial. Two lithic sites in the

eastern US were buried beneath a geotextile filter fabric and crushed blue quarry stone in order to mitigate the impacts of heavy pipeline machinery. The sites were assessed prior to burial and samples taken for later comparison. The sites were monitored throughout the pipeline construction phase (a three- to four-month period). The results show that this artefact-protection method used was successful and that the overall project costs were less than if the sites had been excavated.

Eldridge, M, 1994 *Stabilising erosion at Glenrose wet site, DgRr-6*, Millennia Research for Archaeology Branch, Ministry of Small Business, Tourism and Culture, Victoria, BC, Canada
This report details the steps to stabilise and preserve *in situ* a site found in an intertidal zone. It clearly states what methods were used at the site and how the strategy was implemented, given the constraints of the site's location. A useful example for similar sites in the UK (see also Eldridge 1991 below).

Hunting Technical Services, 1997 Report to Faculty of Archaeology & Cultural History, Vitenskapsmuseet, University of Trondheim, detailing monitoring of archaeological deposits at Schultzgt 3–7, Trondheim, Norway: report R1169, Hunting Technical Services, Hemel Hempstead
Report detailing a programme of deposit monitoring that was established at a redevelopment site in Trondheim. Monitoring of the moisture levels and quality of water within the *in situ* archaeological deposits was undertaken using a range of devices, installed in advance of the site's redevelopment from a car park to retirement flats.

ICOMOS: International Committee on Archaeological Heritage Management, 1994 *Archaeological remains*: in situ *preservation*, Montreal, Canada
The main thrust of these proceedings appears to be concerned with the preservation/conservation of archaeological sites in a museum-setting, as opposed to preservation *in situ* engineered within the construction process. The volume presents papers given at an international conference on archaeological preservation *in situ*, yet there is a glaring lack of British examples. There is one appropriate paper by Dr Robert Thorne: 'Archaeological site preservation as an appropriate and useful management tool', a case study of how to preserve sites along lake edges, using a geotextile material and bank-stabilisation processes, where they are affected by inundation due to dam construction.

Klinger, T C, 1982 *The Mangrum site: mitigation through excavation and preservation*, Arkansas Archaeological Survey
This site report discusses preservation by burial of a site in the USA and is a useful example of monitoring in a mitigation scheme. The Arkansas Archaeological Survey designed a mixed mitigation strategy for a site where a large drainage ditch was to be widened and deepened. The strategy included partial excavation, partial preservation and a monitoring programme. The effec-

tiveness of the burial environment was to be monitored by testing core samples versus those taken of the soils prior to burial, and included comparisons of particle size, unit density, soil pH and moisture content. A monitoring programme was set up to look at the site over a period of 46 years: March 1983, 1988, 1998, 2008 and 2023, with the results to be published in *American Antiquity*. The report also briefly describes four other examples in the USA where burial was used as a preservation method.

Larsson, S, 1995 Nedbrytningen av urbana kulturlager, *Arkeologiska rapporter från Lund, nr 10,* Kulturen, stadshistoriska avdelningen, Box 1095, 221 04 Lund, Sweden
Report on work conducted by the author in Lund on the effect of construction (particularly piling) on *in situ* archaeology.

Legget, R F and Schriever, W R, 1986 Archaeology from a Swiss test boring, *Canadian Geotechnical Journal* 23 (2), 250–2, National Research Council of Canada, Ottawa
A brief article in a geological engineering journal highlighting the importance of close supervision of all aspects of site investigations in areas of archaeological potential. An 'unusual stone' – a stone axe – was noticed by an engineer examining test cores on a lakeside site in Zurich, resulting in the discovery of a significant and important settlement site preserved in the waterlogged lakeside conditions in the late 1970s. Although not strictly a case of preservation *in situ*, the building was redesigned to allow the excavation of the site while the superstructure was built around the archaeologists.

Ljung, J-Å, 1993 *Arkeologisk förundersökning, Kvarteret Sörmlandsbanken,* University of Stockholm, Stockholm, Sweden
Report on a site proposed for redevelopment in Sörmlandsbanken, in which the impact of a 50-year-old basement on underlying cultural deposit is assessed. Visual observations and laboratory analysis are detailed which indicate that dehydration, compression and biodegradation of the archaeological resource has occurred.

Lloyd, E and Mathewson, C C, 1994 Construction loading on an archaeological site, in abstracts from 24–27 October, 1994 annual meeting of the Geological Society of America, Seattle, Washington
Experimental burial to achieve *in situ* preservation of two archaeological sites in Texas. Using pressure cells, the pressures from various loads applied to the ground are reported. An assessment was made of the load experienced by the site before construction (load history), and there is a discussion of machine types and depth of cover over the archaeological remains.

Mathewson, C C, 1993 Preservation of archaeological sites: a joint archaeologist and geologist's responsibility, in abstracts from 25–28 October, 1993 annual meeting of the Geological Society of America, Boston, Massachusetts

Mathewson, C C and Morris, L E, 1995 Intentional burial of two archaeological sites below a highway in Montagu County, Texas: analysis of dynamic loading during construction, *Proceedings of the Symposium on Engineering Geology and Geotechnical Engineering* 31, 260–75
A highly relevant paper on techniques of preservation through burial of archaeological sites, highlighted by an example of practice in the field. Worth reading by anyone thinking about burying a site beneath an embankment/car park, etc.

Peacock, E, 1996 Myntverkstedet I Erkebispegården: Del II Tilstand og KonseringsforslagI, *Konserveringsseksjonen,* Vtenskapsmuseet, NTNU, Trondheim, Norway
A report discussing the reburied remains of a *myntverksted* (mint) at the site of the Erkebispegården (Royal Palace), Trondheim, Norway. A temporary reburial system, comprising geotextile, polyurethane and sediment, had been placed over the *in situ* remains following their discovery in 1992. In 1996 this was lifted and an assessment made of the underlying remains as part of the design of a long-term preservation strategy.

Salvadori, M G, 1976 Historical sites and the construction engineer, *Journal of the Construction Division* 102 (2), 295–301
Although out of date, it is interesting to read because it represents a 'call to arms' to construction engineers to face the fact that construction is mostly responsible for the vast majority of the destruction of archaeological (and palaeontological) sites in the US (it also includes some rather alarming statistics). The author, a civil engineer, calls for greater awareness and cooperation between the construction industry and the archaeologists/palaeontologists.

Thorne, R M, 1995 *In-place archaeological site conservation and stabilization bibliography,* National Clearinghouse for Archaeological Site Stabilization, Centre for Archaeological Research, University of Mississippi
This is an ongoing comprehensive bibliography of American articles about *in situ* preservation. It is divided into four sections: philosophy; technical support; management recommendations; and practical applications. Updated versions are available on request from the research centre.

Weakly, W F, 1980 Preservation of historic sites during construction, *Journal of the Construction Division* 106 (3), 351–4
A short US article published in a construction industry journal highlighting the necessity of early integration of the concept of preservation of archaeological remains within a construction programme. Uses a construction project in Colorado as an example of how to accomplish this. States that taking on board the concerns of preserving historic/archaeological remains so that they are 'adequately taken into account ... does not in any way interfere with project development, nor does it add excessive costs'.

D4.0 Mitigation theory and preservation *in situ* trends

Biddle, M, 1994 *What future for British archaeology?*, Archaeology in Britain conference 1994, Oxford
Opening address of the conference, in which the background to PPG 16 is summarised. Reference is made to the problems of applying the guidance from PPG 16, made in the context of possible construction impacts that can occur to *in situ* remains when a site is developed. Examples of construction impacts are taken from Norway and the UK.

Dixon, K A, 1971 Archaeological site preservation: the neglected alternative to destruction, *Pacific Coast Archaeological Society Quarterly* 7 (4)

Fitting, J E, 1981 The cost of mitigation, *Contract Abstracts and CRM Archaeology* 2 (1), 10–12

Ford, R I, 1983 The archaeological conservancy, inc.: the goal is site preservation, *American Archaeology* 3 (3), 221–4

McGill, G, 1995 *Building on the past: a guide to the archaeology and development process*, London
A detailed introductory textbook giving information on all aspects of the development process and how it affects archaeology. It should be required reading for all planners, archaeologists, developers and engineers as it clearly sets out all sides of the process culminating in preservation by record or preservation *in situ* (or a combination of both). There are three main sections: (i) archaeological considerations; (ii) public controls; and (iii) development considerations. These sections are further subdivided into more detail with references for further reading. Under (ii), chapter 13 'Design considerations' is of particular interest to this study. This chapter gives details on the different methods of site investigation used from an engineer's/developer's point of view; the types of foundations used; the need to adapt the building design to protect the archaeological remains *in situ*; methods of incorporating archaeological remains into the building design; and finally, the issue of reconstructing the past in terms of the preserved *in situ* archaeology (ie the Jorvik Centre in York).

Miller, P, 1994 Dig or pile? *Planning Week* 2 (43), viii–ix
A brief article outlining GIS work carried out by York Archaeological Trust and York University. A GIS database is used to anticipate the presence of archaeology under proposed development sites and to highlight potential difficulties early in the planning process. On the basis of the GIS information, in conjunction with archaeological site-evaluation data, the principal archaeologist can then work with the developer to design a specific mitigation strategy for the site in question.

Oxley, J, 1993 Everything (??) you wanted to know about mitigation strategies but were afraid to ask ... *The Field Archaeologist* 19, 383
Overview of one session at the Institute of Field Archaeologists' ABC'93 conference. The paper briefly describes what a mitigation strategy should entail, and explains the reasoning behind Ove Arup's decision to recommend in York an acceptable 5 per cent loss of a site's archaeology due to construction processes. An example in London at Bruce House, Covent Garden, is used to show that cooperation between archaeologists and developers/engineers can bring about a successful outcome with regard to the archaeology (even at a late stage in the development's progress). The paper emphasises the need for good communication between all parties involved in a development, and the need for the early inclusion of archaeological expertise.

Raab, L M, 1981 Getting first things first: taming the mitigation monster, *Contract Abstracts and CRM Archaeology* 2, 7–9

Schiffer, M B, 1987 *Formation processes of the archaeological record*, Albuquerque, New Mexico
A clear and succinct textbook approach to the formation of archaeological sites through cultural and environmental means. The book as a whole is of interest here, in particular chapter 6 'Disturbance processes', where the concepts of assessing and mitigating impacts to archaeological sites are discussed.

Schiffer, M B and Gummerman, G J, 1977 *Conservation archaeology: a guide for cultural resource management studies*, London
A volume of papers concerning topical issues in contract archaeology in the US in the late 1970s, ie mitigation of impacts, aimed primarily at the contract archaeologist. The authors clearly state that they are attempting to present 'an ethic, a method and to some extent a theory for archaeologists engaged in contract work ... a statement of philosophy buttressed by case studies'. Topics of interest here include those on predictive modelling of the archaeological resource; assessing significance; forecasting impacts; and mitigation.

Thompson, G, 1997 The impact of engineering on buried archaeological artefacts in the UK, unpublished dissertation for the Soil Mechanics MSc, Imperial College, London
This assessment of engineering impacts on buried archaeology describes the chemical composition of artefacts, their physical location (ie environment) and the effect that certain types of impacts (piling, excavations, tunnelling and embankments) can have on archaeology. Presents an overview of current knowledge. Concludes that the full assessment of archaeological impacts from the outset of a development project can have significant reductions in costs and time delays, compared with dealing with unexpected archaeology during the construction process.

Wainwright, G J, 1989 Archaeology in towns, *Conservation Bulletin* 9, 1–2
A short pre-PPG 16 article on the necessity of preservation *in situ*. Emphasises the roles that planners and the planning process play in the decision to preserve *in situ*. Also stresses the need for early, effective cooperation and discussion between all parties concerned, ie the developer, planners and archaeologists. Cites events in York and London (1989) as examples where such cooperation is most evident.

D5.0 Technical and scientific research

D5.1 US Army Engineering Corps / US Federal Departments

Bowie, A J, 1981 *Investigations of vegetation for stabilising eroding streambanks: streambank stability, appendix C,* report submitted to the US Army Engineer District, Vicksburg, by the USDA Sedimentation Laboratory, Oxford, Mississippi

Carrell, T, Rayl, S and Lenihan, D, 1976 *The effects of freshwater inundation of archaeological sites through reservoir construction: a literature search,* US Department of Interior, National Park Service, Cultural Resources Management Division, Washington DC

Henderson, J E and Sheilds Jr, F D, 1984 *Environmental features for streambank protection projects,* Technical report E-84-11, US Army Engineer Waterways Experiment Station, Vicksburg, Mississippi

Jones, C W, 1970 *Effect of a polymer on the properties of soil cement,* Bureau of Reclamation report no. RFC-OCF-20-18, Denver, Colorado

Keown, M P, Oswalt, N R, Perry, E B and Dardeau Jr, E A, 1977 *Literature survey and preliminary evaluation of streambank protection methods,* Technical report H-77-9, US Army Engineer Waterways Experiment Station, Vicksburg, Mississippi

Keown, M P and Dardeau Jr, E A, 1980 *Utilisation of filter fabric for streambank protection applications,* Technical report HL-80-12, US Army Engineer Waterways Experiment Station, Vicksburg, Mississippi

Kinter, E B, 1975 *Development and evaluation of chemical soil stabilizers,* Federal Highway Administration report no. FHWA-RD-75-17, Washington DC

Lynott, M, 1984 *Stabilization plan: Clyde Creek archaeological site (2ILS35),* Midwest Archaeological Centre, National Park, Lincoln, Nebraska

Mathewson, C C (ed), 1987 *Proceedings of the interdisciplinary workshop on the physical-chemical-biological processes affecting archaeological sites,* US Army Engineer Waterways Experiment Station, Vicksburg, Mississippi

Mathewson, C, Gonzalez, T and Eblen, J S, 1992 *Burial as a method of archaeological site protection,* Contract report EL-92-1, US Army Engineer Waterways Experiment Station, Vicksburg, Mississippi

National Park Service, 1976 *Policy on non-aqueous burial of archaeological sites,* Mem L76-MQ, National Park Service, Washington DC

Thorne, R M, 1988 *Guidelines for the organisation of archaeological site stabilisation projects: a modelled approach,* Technical report EL-88-8, US Army Engineer Waterways Experiment Station, Vicksburg, Mississippi
In response to the growing concern in the US regarding preservation *in situ* issues, a study was implemented in the mid 1980s which looked at professional archaeologists' knowledge, awareness and implementation of preservation techniques. As a result of the study's findings the author presents here a nine-staged model of how to go about implementing a preservation strategy. The paper stresses the need for archaeologists to disseminate their data on preservation *in situ* techniques so that others can use and/or build on their results, also the need for monitoring of the site to evaluate the overall effectiveness of the scheme.

Thorne, R M, 1989 *Intentional site burial: a technique to protect against natural or mechanical loss,* Technical brief no. 5, Archaeological Assistance Program, Centre for Archaeological Research, University of Mississippi, US Department of the Interior
Second technical brief on site stabilisation and maintenance of archaeological sites. Though the areas discussed are more comprehensively covered elsewhere (see further papers by Thorne and by C C Mathewson), the paper does include a short annotated bibliography.

Thorne, R, Fay, P M and Hester, J J, 1987 *Archaeological site preservation techniques: a preliminary review,* Technical report EL-87-3, US Army Engineer Waterways Experiment Station, Vicksburg, Mississippi

US Army Corps of Engineers, 1992 *The archaeological sites protection and preservation notebook,* Environmental Impact Research Program, Waterways Experiment Station, Vicksburg, Mississippi

This is a compendium of research into preservation *in situ* techniques carried out by the US Army Corps of Engineers. It has sections on impacts; site burial; structural stabilisation; soil and rock stabilisation; vegetative stabilisation; camouflage and diversionary tactics; site surveillance; stabilisation of existing structures; faunal and floral control; signs; and, finally, inundation. There is also a bibliography of all research carried out by the Army Corps that is related to site preservation and protection.

Wilson, R L, 1976 *Professional consideration surrounding non-aqueous burial of archaeological sites,* Inter-agency Archaeological Programme Memorandum no. 4, supplement no. 1: Washington DC

D5.2 UK technical papers

Briggs, D E G and Evershed, R P, 1996 The chitin files: fossil cuticle, a complex chemical conundrum, *Ancient Biomolecules Initiative Newsletter* 3, 61–4, Natural Environment Research Council
Discussion of the factors responsible for the survival and degradation of beetle remains.

Canti, M G, 1995 A study of the properties of a proposed alternative to Buckland sand for site reburial, Ancient Monuments Laboratory report 7/95, English Heritage, London
Report detailing methodology and result of an investigation into particle size characteristics, soluble salts and iron coatings on samples of Buckland silica sand and one other silica sand. Use of silica sands for site reburial as part of an *in situ* preservation scheme is discussed and the two sand sources are given.

Caple, C and Dungmore, D, 1996 Investigations into waterlogged burial environments, in *Archaeological science 1995* (ed E A Slater and A Sinclair), Oxford

Carrott, J, Hall, A, Issitt, M, Kenward, H, Large, F, Milles, A and Usai, R, 1996 Suspected accelerated *in situ* decay of delicate bioarchaeological remains: a case study from medieval York, Environmental Archaeology Unit report 96/15, York
Report of a research project into sediment characteristics and preservation conditions of organic deposits at 44–45 Parliament Street, York. Discusses impact on archaeological deposits of dewatering that may have occurred during construction of a previous but now demolished building, and down-movement of salts from an overlying concrete slab.

Collinson, M E, Finch, P and Scott, A C, 1996 Fossil plant cuticles – what are they?, *Ancient Biomolecules Initiative Newsletter* 3, 65–70, Natural Environment Research Council
Research into the environmental requirements responsible for the preservation of plant cuticles.

Corfield, M, 1996 Preventative conservation for archaeological sites, in *Archaeological conservation and its consequences* (ed A Roy and P Smith), 32–7, International Institute for the Conservation of Historic and Artistic Works, London
Review of English Heritage projects designed to establish the baseline for preservation in different environments. Focus of paper is on research into *in situ* preservation of organic materials in waterlogged environments. Discusses the soil and water characteristics of sites, and the parameters that can be monitored, eg hydraulic conductivity, water quality and water chemistry.

English Heritage, 1994 An environmental evaluation at the Rose Theatre, Southwark, London, Central Archaeology Services report CAS site 441, English Heritage, London
A limited programme of site investigation was conducted on the site of the reburied Rose Theatre remains. The temporary preservation system installed over the remains in 1989 was inspected to assess its continuing performance, and a report of the general site conditions was produced. This included a material investigation of redundant concrete piles and the efflorescence forming on them, an investigation of the underlying soils, and an investigation of possible gas generation.

Goodburn-Brown, D and Hughes, R, 1996 A review of some conservation procedures for the reburial of archaeological sites in London, in *Proceedings of the IIC 16th international congress, Copenhagen: Archaeological conservation and its consequences,* Copenhagen, Denmark
Review of several sites on which the Museum of London have been involved in the installation of reburial preservation schemes using sand and Terram. Sites include the shallow Saxon cremations and inhumations at Park Lane in Croydon, and the Bronze Age ard marks at Wolseley Street in Southwark.

Hunting Land & Environment, 1996 Study of sands for use in the preservation backfill at Anchor Terrace car park, 1–15 Southwark Bridge Road, London SE1: report R1112, Hunting Technical Services, Hemel Hempstead, Hertfordshire
Study to investigate the suitability of nine different sands for use as a backfill material in a preservation *in situ* scheme on a site containing remains associated with the Globe Theatre. Details are given of the chemical techniques used to investigate the various sand's iron content, and reference is made to an earlier study of two sands by English Heritage (see also Canti 1995 above).

Wagner, D, Kropp, M, Abelskamp-Boos, K A N, Dakoronia, F, Earl, N, Ferguson, C, Fischer, W R, Hills, C C, Kars, H, Leenheer, R and Meijers, R, 1997 *Soil archive classification of European excavation sites in terms of impacts of conservability of archaeological heritage,* European Commission Contract EV5V-CT94-0516, Brussels, Belgium
A project funded by the European Commission under the

Environment and Climate programme with the primary objective of a 'soil archive' classification with regard to the corrosion state of metal artefacts. Iron and bronze artefacts were used as 'tracer artefacts' and the description of their present state within sites in combination with the knowledge of degradation mechanisms was used to set up a user-manual with guidelines for the categorisation of excavation sites, and to propose corrosion-relevant preventative countermeasures.

D5.3 Others

Abdul-Kareem, A W and McRae, S G, 1984 The effects on topsoil of long-term storage in stockpiles, *Plant and Soil* 76, 357–63

Aldrich, H P, 1979 Preserving the foundations of older buildings: the importance of ground water levels, *Technology and Conservation Magazine* 4 (2), 32–7

Barton, M E, 1995 The Bargate Centre, Southampton: engineering, geological and geohydrological aspects of the excavation for basement construction, in *Engineering geology of construction* (ed M Eddleston et al), Geological Society Engineering Geology special publication 10, 67–77
A case history of the Bargate Centre where a cut-off wall, provided by an anchored secant bored pile wall, was required to construct a basement to between 6 and 7m below ground level. Two potential construction impacts from this project on the nearby medieval town walls were identified: ground stains induced by the excavation, and settlement induced by groundwater lowering. Both construction impacts were assessed using pre- and post-construction piezometer water-level data. The paper recommended continuous monitoring of piezometers and also greater use of historical research. For example, it was found that modification of groundwater seepage had occurred by the double moats which surrounded the medieval town walls.

Bell, M, Fowler, P J and Hillson, S W (eds), 1996 *The experimental earthwork project 1960–1992*, Council for British Archaeology research report 100
The Overton Down and Wareham experimental earthworks were set up in 1960 in order to test the preservation of organic and inorganic materials and assess processes of weathering over time (see Section 3.1.2 above).

Briuer, F L and Niquette, C M, 1983 *Military impacts to archaeological sites*, Paper on file at Cultural Resource Analysts, Inc

Coles, B, 1995 *Wetland management: a survey for English Heritage*, WARP Occasional Paper 9, Exeter
Though not directly associated with impacts from construction activities, there is reference made to the *in situ* preservation of archaeological remains in wetland environments. This is a fragile environment which is susceptible to change as a result of ground disturbances (eg drainage).

Cronyn, J M, 1990 *The elements of archaeological conservation*, London
The basics of archaeological conservation techniques, primarily post-excavation. However, chapter 2 is of interest here for its background information on agents of deterioration and preservation.

Dowman, E A, 1970 *Conservation in field archaeology*, London
Out of date, but Part One, 'Environment and its effects' (ie soils and particular environments) could be useful.

Eldridge, M T, 1991 *Engineering solutions to erosion of the Glenrose wet site component*, BC Archaeology Branch, Provincial Government of British Columbia, Victoria, BC, Canada

Fay, P M, 1987 Archaeological site stabilization in the Tennessee River Valley – phase III, *Archaeological Papers of the Centre for Archaeological Research* 7, University of Mississippi, Tennessee Valley Authority Publications in Anthropology 49, Norris, Tennessee

Ferguson, A and Turnbull, C, 1980 Ministers Island Seawall: an experiment in archaeological site preservation, in *Proceedings of the 1980 conference on the future of the archaeology in the Maritime Provinces* (ed D M Schemabuku), Occasional Papers in Anthropology 8, Department of Anthropology, St Mary's University, Halifax, Nova Scotia

French, C, 1995 *Dewatering, desiccation and erosion: an appraisal of water and fen in the East Anglian fenlands*, Department of Archaeology, University of Cambridge
Discussion of processes and timescales involved in dewatering and the actual destruction of the archaeological resource. Reference made to various research projects that are attempting to assess the perceived impact to the preservation of organic remains from gravels extraction.

French, C and Davis, M, 1994 *The long-term hydrological monitoring of relict landscapes at Willingham gravel quarry, Cambridgeshire: project design*, Department of Archaeology, Cambridge/Hunting Land & Environment, Hemel Hempstead, Hertfordshire

French, C and Taylor, M, 1985 Desiccation and destruction: the immediate effects of de-watering at Etton, Cambridgeshire, *Oxford Journal of Archaeology* 4 (2), 139–55
Paper presenting the first results from a long-term project to monitor the impact from gravel extraction on groundwater conditions. The pumping of groundwater in a field adjacent to the Etton middle Neolithic causewayed enclosure is discussed and the effects of dewatering on deposits of wood in the enclosure ditch.

Garfinkel, A and Lister, B L, 1983 Effects of high embankment construction on archaeological materials: report no. FHWA/CA/TL-83/02, Office of Transportation Laboratory, California Department of Transportation
This paper presents the results of a preliminary study conducted by the California Department of Transportation in the late 1970s which examined the effects of burying an archaeological site under a 75ft embankment. Their results indicated that there was some compaction of the surrounding stratigraphy and inconsequential damage to fragile artefacts, while stone artefacts were generally unaffected (these results are obviously dependent on the individual site conditions). The conclusions and recommendations are presented clearly and are of use to the practitioner contemplating placing a site under an embankment in order to preserve it *in situ*.

Goffer, Z, 1980 *Archaeological chemistry: a sourcebook on the applications of chemistry to archaeology,* New York

Gonzalez, T, 1989 Study of soils buried under embankments to determine the potential of burial as a preservation technique for archaeological sites, unpublished MSc thesis, Texas A&M University, College Station, Texas

Gyrisco, G, 1981 Cases of direct and incidental protection of archaeological sites through easements, *Contract Abstracts and CRM Archaeology* 2 (1), 32–5

Hughes, R, 1990 A note on the potential conservation techniques for the Globe Theatre structural remins and associated *in situ* soils, unpublished report prepared for the Museum of London

Hunter, F and Currie, J A, 1956 Structural changes during bulk soil storage, *Journal of Soil Science* 7, 75–80

Hunter, K, 1980 A study to determine the possibility of testing archaeological soils for factors influencing the preservation of artefacts, unpublished dissertation for Diploma in Archaeological Conservation, University of Durham

Johnson, P, 1982 Perspectives on archaeological site capping, *Contract Abstracts and CRM Archaeology* 3 (1), 41–2

Mathewson, C C and Gonzalez, T, 1988 Protection and preservation of archaeological sites through burial, in *Engineering geology of ancient works, monuments and historic sites: preservation and protection* (ed P G Marinos and G C Koukis), Rotterdam, Netherlands

Introduces the concept of a site-decay model, including a discussion on the processes (physical, chemical and biological) affecting site decay.

Ove Arup & Partners, 1989 The Rose Theatre, unpublished report prepared for the Theatres Trust

Podany, J, Neville, A and Martha, D, 1993 Preservation of excavated mosaics by reburial: evaluation of some traditional and newly developed materials and techniques, *Proceedings of the 5th conference of the International Committee for the Conservation of Mosaics,* 1–19, Conimbriga, Portugal
This paper reviews the design and implementation of reburial strategies as a means of preserving excavated mosaics. Included is a comparison between reburial by simply replacing the excavated material over the mosaic, and the use of imported natural materials or newly developed synthetic products, such as geotextiles. A list of the main characteristics that a backfill material should possess are given.

Skinner, S M, 1989 Experimental study to assess the effects of compaction and pressure on artefacts in archaeological sites, unpublished report prepared for Texas Eastern Gas Pipeline Company, by Archaeological Services Consultants, Inc, Columbus, Ohio

Snethkamp, P E, 1983 Archaeological investigations on San Miguel Island, 1982: erosion control and site stabilisation treatments, draft report submitted to the Western Region, National Park Service, San Francisco

Thorne, R M, 1985 Preservation is a use: archaeological site stabilisation: an experimental program in the Tennessee River Valley, *Archaeological Papers of the Centre for Archaeological Research* 4, University of Mississippi, Tennessee Valley Authority Publications in Anthropology 40, Norris, Tennessee

Ward, R C and Robinson, M, 1990 *Principles of hydrology,* 3rd edition, London

Watkinson, D (ed), 1987 *First aid for finds,* RESCUE/UKIC Archaeology Section, London
As the title suggests, this handbook is primarily for post-excavation. However, Section 1.2 details the buried environments that are typically found in the UK and how they may affect archaeological remains.

GLOSSARY

allowable bearing capacity The foundation pressure the ground can carry without undue deformation.

anaerobic A condition where oxygen is excluded (aerobic is the opposite state).

anchor Something restraining movement, such as a bolt screwed into concrete or, on a larger scale, a tie rod holding back a retaining wall.

aquiclude (aquitard) A geological formation of low *permeability*, that delays the flow of water from an aquifer. It may itself contain a large quantity of water, but gives it up too slowly to be considered an aquifer.

archaeological feature A generic term for the cut, or excavated remains of human activity (eg pits, ditches).

archaeological remains/resource Term encompassing the full repertoire of archaeological materials on a site (eg features, artefacts, environmental remains).

artefact An object made or modified by man.

auger A boring tool used for extracting soil.

backacter (backhow, drag shovel, trench hoe) A mechanical excavator that digs towards the machine.

barrette The short elements that join to make a diaphragm wall.

beam A structural member designed to resist loads which bend it. Beams are usually of wood, steel or reinforced concrete.

bill of quantities A list of numbered items, each describing the quantity, measurement unit and sometimes the price of work to be done in a civil-engineering project.

borehole A hole driven into the ground to get information about the strata and obtain samples.

buried soil An undisturbed ancient land surface, protected by an existing monument or by an accumulation of later deposits.

cantilever An overhanging beam fixed at one end and free at the overhanging (cantilevered) end.

chippings For general construction, crushed stone from 3 to 25mm.

cohesion of/cohesive soil The stickiness of clay or silt, absent from sands, characteristic of clays.

competent Soils that are stable and relatively strong.

cone of depression Cone shape of the water table around a well being pumped. A similar cone or crater is formed around a structure built on clay or other compressible soil as the soil slowly squeezes under the load of the structure.

core The cylinder of rock or soil or concrete cut out by a diamond drill or soil sampler.

crib wall A retaining wall built of stone-filled gabions or precast concrete units or timbers stacked on top of each other.

cutting, cut An excavation for carrying a canal, railway, road or pipeline below ground level in the open.

drilling fluid/mud The mud which is pumped into the drill pipe in rotary drilling.

environmental remains Remains that provide information about prevailing contemporary ecological conditions (eg wood, charcoal, pollen, seeds, molluscs, insects, faunal remains).

failure A condition at which a structure reaches a limit state (conditions in which a structure would become unfit for use).

firm clay/firm silt A clay or silt which can be dug with a spade and moulded by firmly squeezing in the hand.

fly ash Extremely fine ash from the burning of pulverised coal. When it has more than 90 per cent silica it may be used as a pozzolan in concrete.

french drain A filter drain or field drain (unsocketed, earthenware, porous concrete, perforated plastic pipe) laid end to end in a trench and surrounded by a graded filter or gravel.

gabion A rectangular steel mesh basket filled with rocks, used with others for building a free-draining retaining wall.

geogrid A non-woven geotextile with large holes on a rectangular layout.

geotextile Corrosion-resistant/non-biodegradable plastic sheet which is permeable (unlike a geomembrane).

hard-core Hard lumps of stone, gravel, brick, furnace slag, old concrete, etc.

inspection chamber A shallow pit of small diameter or a shaft, through which a sewer or drain can be inspected and rodded.

joint A discontinuity in rock, where it breaks easily.

kentledge Loading to give weight and thus stability to a crane, to provide a reaction over a jack, to push down a plate in the plate-bearing test, or to test a bearing pile.

lean concrete Concrete containing little cement and usually little water.

load The weight carried by a structure or foundations.

load-bearing wall A wall which carries a load in addition to its own weight and the wind force on it.

made ground Ground which has been raised by fill, ie introduced soil or other material.

mechanical excavator A self-propelled digging machine.

microtunnel Any machine-made tunnel too small for a person to work in.

moisture content The weight of water in a soil mass divided by the weight of dry solids and multiplied by 100.

mole plough A vertical knife blade carrying a horizontal bullet shape at its lower end that is pulled through the ground.

moling Microtunnelling, pipe renewal or using a mole plough.

permeability In cm/s or other unit of speed, the rate of diffusion of a fluid under pressure through soil, concrete, etc.

piezometer tube An open-topped tube (standpipe) for measuring water pressures.

piping Subsurface erosion by the movement of water.

pulverised fuel ash see **fly ash**

reinforced concrete Concrete containing reinforcement consisting of steel rods or mesh.

sand drain A boring through a clay or silty soil, filled with sand or gravel to enable the soil to drain more easily.

settlement/subsidence Downward movement of the ground surface.

shearing Failure of materials under shear.

shear modulus It is equal to the shear stress divided by the shear strain.

shear stress The shear force (ie load acting across a beam near its support) per unit of cross-sectioned area, expressed in kN/m^2 like other stresses.

slab Any large thin area of concrete such as a wall, a road or a roof. If suspended it is the thin part of a reinforced-concrete floor between beams or supporting walls.

slurry Any fluid mixture of fine solids and water, particularly one which contains cement or bentonite.

sodium silicate $Na_2 SiO_3$. A white soluble crystalline salt, used in the manufacture of cement.

soil nailing Driving or grouting small-diameter rods into holes bored in soil.

stanchion A vertical steel strut. A concrete strut is usually called a column.

stratigraphy Position of deposits/remains in a profile. The interpretation of archaeological stratification relies on the geological Law of Superposition: where one deposit overlies another, the upper must have accumulated later in time than the lower, which could not have been inserted beneath a layer already there.

strength The strength of a material is measured by its greatest safe working stress. The strength of a structural part is its ability to resist the loads which fall on it.

stress (mech) The force on a member divided by the area which carries the force, formerly expressed in psi, now in N/mm^2, Mpa, etc.

sump A pit in which water collects before being baled or pumped out.

superstructure The visible part of a structure; that part above the substructure.

surcharging Any load acting on the ground surface.

surfactant A substance when emulsified disperses, dissolves or penetrates other substances, or makes them froth.

tension A pulling force or stress.

toe level A toe line, the level to which the feet of piles are driven.

trémie A sheet-metal hopper with a pipe leading out of the bottom of it, used for placing concrete under water.

trench drain see **french drain**

underpin To provide new, deeper support under a wall or column without removing the superstructure, so as to allow the load on the building to be increased, or to allow the ground inside or outside it to be lowered, or to prevent settlement of the foundation. It is the construction of foundations for a building which exists.

viscosity The resistance of a fluid to flow.

Sources:

Bray, W and Trump, D, 1982 *The Penguin dictionary of archaeology* (2nd edition), Harmondsworth

Scott, J S, 1991 *The Penguin dictionary of civil engineering* (4th edition), Harmondsworth

REFERENCES

Abdul-Kareem, A W and McRae, S G, 1984 The effects on topsoil of long-term storage in stockpiles, *Plant and Soil* 76, 357–63

Ardito, A J, 1994 Reducing the effects of heavy equipment compaction through *in situ* archaeological site preservation, *Antiquity* 68, 816–20

Ayre, J, 1997 *Bull Wharf, Upper Thames Street, EC4, City of London: archaeological works 1989–1997*, Museum of London Archaeology Service, London

Bardos, R P, Nathanail, C P and Weenk, A, 2000 *Assessing the wider environment value of remediating land contamination: a review*, R&D Technical report P238, Environment Agency R&D Dissemination Centre, c/o WRc, Franklin Road, Swindon

Bell, M, Fowler, P J and Hillson, S W (eds), 1996 *The experimental earthwork project 1960–1992*, Council for British Archaeology research report 100

Biddle, M, 1994 *What future for British archaeology?*, Archaeology in Britain conference 1994, Oxford

Blyth, F G H and de Freitas, M H, 1984 *A geology for engineers* (7th edition), London

Bowles, J E, 1996 *Foundation analysis and design* (5th edition), New York

BRE: Building Research Establishment, 1986 *Mini-piling for low-rise buildings*, Digest 313, Building Research Establishment, Garston, Watford

Breeze, D, 1993 Ancient monuments legislation, in *Archaeological resource management in the UK* (ed J Hunter and I Ralston), 44–55, Stroud

Briggs, D E G and Evershed, R P, 1996 The chitin files: fossil cuticle, a complex chemical conundrum, *Ancient Biomolecules Initiative Newsletter* 3, 61–4, Natural Environment Research Council

Broms, B B, 1981 *Precast piling practice*, London

BS: British Standards Institution, BS 8004: 1986 *Code of practice for foundations*, British Standards Institution, London

BS: British Standards Institution, BS 1377: 1990 *Methods of test for soils for civil engineering purposes*, British Standards Institution, London

BS: British Standards Institution, BS 5930: 1999 *Code of practice for site investigations*, British Standards Institution, London

BS: British Standards Institution, BS 10175: 2001 *Code of practice: the investigation of potentially contaminated sites*, British Standards Institution, London

Canti, M G, 1995 A study of the properties of a proposed alternative to Buckland sand for site reburial, Ancient Monuments Laboratory report 7/95, English Heritage, London

Caple, C and Dungmore, D, 1996 Investigations into water-logged burial environments, in *Archaeological science 1995* (ed E A Slater and A Sinclair), Oxford

Carbognin, L and Gatto, P, 1986 An overview of the subsidence of Venice, *International Association of Hydrological Sciences Publication* 151, 321–8

Carrott, J, Hall, A, Issitt, M, Kenward, H, Large, F, Milles, A and Usai, R, 1996 Suspected accelerated *in situ* decay of delicate bioarchaeological remains: a case study from medieval York, Environmental Archaeology Unit report 96/15, York

Charles, J A, 1993 *Building on fill: geotechnical aspects*, Building Research Establishment, Garston, Watford

Chudley, R and Greeno, R, 2001 *Building construction handbook* (4th edition), Oxford

CIRIA, 1995 *Remedial treatment for contaminated land, Volume I: Introduction and guide*, special publication 101, Construction Industry Research & Information Association (CIRIA), London

CIRIA, 1995 *Remedial treatment for contaminated land, Volume II: Decommissioning, decontamination and demolition*, special publication 102, Construction Industry Research & Information Association (CIRIA), London

CIRIA, 1995 *Remedial treatment for contaminated land, Volume III: Site investigation and assessment*, special publication 103, Construction Industry Research & Information Association (CIRIA), London

CIRIA, 1995a *Remedial treatment for contaminated land, Volume IV: Classification and selection of remedial methods*, special publication 104, Construction Industry Research & Information Association (CIRIA), London

CIRIA, 1995 *Remedial treatment for contaminated land, Volume V: Excavation and disposal*, special publication 105, Construction Industry Research & Information Association (CIRIA), London

CIRIA, 1995 *Remedial treatment for contaminated land, Volume VI:*

Containment and hydraulic measures, special publication 106, Construction Industry Research & Information Association (CIRIA), London

CIRIA, 1995 *Remedial treatment for contaminated land, Volume VII: Ex-situ remedial methods for soils, sludges and sediments*, special publication 107, Construction Industry Research & Information Association (CIRIA), London

CIRIA, 1995 *Remedial treatment for contaminated land, Volume VIII: Ex-situ remedial methods for contaminated groundwater and other liquids*, special publication 108, Construction Industry Research & Information Association (CIRIA), London

CIRIA, 1995b *Remedial treatment for contaminated land, Volume IX: In-situ methods of remediation*, special publication 109, Construction Industry Research & Information Association (CIRIA), London

CIRIA, 1995 *Remedial treatment for contaminated land, Volume X: Special situations*, special publication 110, Construction Industry Research & Information Association (CIRIA), London

CIRIA, 1995 *Remedial treatment for contaminated land, Volume XI: Planning and management*, special publication 111, Construction Industry Research & Information Association (CIRIA), London

CIRIA, 1995 *Remedial treatment for contaminated land, Volume XII: Policy and legislation*, special publication 112, Construction Industry Research & Information Association (CIRIA), London

CIRIA, 1996 *Crane stability on site: an introductory guide*, special publication 131, Construction Industry Research & Information Association (CIRIA), London

Clayton, C R I, Simons, N E and Matthews, M C, 1995 *Site investigation*, Oxford

Cole, K W, 1988 *ICE works construction guides: foundations*, London

Coles, B, 1995 *Wetland management: a survey for English Heritage*, WARP Occasional Paper 9, Exeter

Collinson, M E, Finch, P and Scott, A C, 1996 Fossil plant cuticles – what are they?, *Ancient Biomolecules Initiative Newsletter* 3, 65–70, Natural Environment Research Council

Corfield, M, 1996 Preventative conservation for archaeological sites, in *Archaeological conservation and its consequences* (ed A Roy and P Smith), 32–7, International Institute for the Conservation of Historic and Artistic Works, London

Corfield, M, Hinton, P, Nixon, T and Pollard, M (eds), 1998 *Preserving archaeological remains in situ: proceedings of the conference of 1st to 3rd April 1996*, Museum of London and University of Bradford, London

Cronyn, J M, 1990 *The elements of archaeological conservation*, London

Dalwood, C H, Buteux, V A and Darlington, J, 1994 Excavations at Farrier Street and other sites north of the city wall, Worcester 1988–1992, *Transactions of the Worcestershire Archaeological Society* 3 (14), 75–114

Darvill, T, 1996 Review of G McGill *Building on the past: a guide to the archaeology and development process*, in *The Field Archaeologist* 23

Darvill, T and Fulton, A K, 1998 *MARS: The monuments at risk survey in England, 1995: main report*, Bournemouth University and English Heritage, Bournemouth and London

Davis, M, 1994 Rose Theatre environmental monitoring programme: investigation of site conditions and repair or replacement of monitoring points: report R898, Hunting Land & Environment, Hemel Hempstead, Hertfordshire

Davis, M, 1996 Archaeological deposit monitoring at 44/45 Parliament Street, York: report detailing the installation of monitoring points: report R1052, Hunting Land & Environment, Hemel Hempstead, Hertfordshire

Davis, M, 1998 *In situ* monitoring of wet archaeological environments: a review of available monitoring technologies, in Corfield et al 1998, 21–5

DETR: Department of the Environment, Transport and the Regions, 2000 *DETR Circular. Environmental Protection Act 1990: Part IIA Contaminated Land*, London

DoE: Department of the Environment, 1989 *Environmental assessment: a guide to the procedures*, London

DoE: Department of the Environment, 1990 *Archaeology and planning*, Planning Policy Guidance PPG 16, London

DoE: Department of the Environment, 1992 *The use of land for amenity purposes: a summary of requirements*, London

Dowman, E A, 1970 *Conservation in field archaeology*, London

Edwards, R, 1998 The effects of changes in groundwater on the survival of buried metal artefacts, in Corfield et al 1998, 86–92

English Heritage, 1992 *Development plan policies for archaeology*, English Heritage, London

English Heritage, 1994 An environmental evaluation at the Rose Theatre, Southwark, London, Central Archaeology Services report CAS site 441, English Heritage, London

English Heritage, 1998 *Greater London Archaeology Advisory Service: archaeological guidance papers*, English Heritage, London

Evans, D, 1994 *Blue Bridge Lane: a concise report on an archaeological evaluation*, York Archaeological Trust, York

Fleming, W K, Weltman, A J, Randolph, M F and Elson, W K, 1994 *Piling engineering* (2nd edition), London

Freeze, R A and Banner, J, 1970 The mechanism of natural groundwater recharge and discharge 2: laboratory column experiments and field measurements, *Water Resources Research* 6, 138–55

French, C and Davis, M, 1994 *The long-term hydrological monitoring of relict landscapes at Willingham gravel quarry, Cambridgeshire: project design*, Department of Archaeology, Cambridge/Hunting Land & Environment, Hemel Hempstead, Hertfordshire

French, C A I, Davis, M and Heathcote, S, 1999 Hydrological monitoring of an alluvial landscape in the Lower Great

Ouse Valley, Cambridgeshire: interim results of the first three years, *Environmental Archaeology* 4, 41–56

Gaffney, V and Tingle, M, 1984 The tyranny of the site: method and theory in field survey, *Scottish Archaeological Review* 3, 134–40

Griffiths, M, 1995 *Blue Bridge Lane: mitigation strategy*, Mike Griffiths and Associates, Darlington

Henn, R W, 1996 *Practical guide to grouting of underground structures*, London

Hillson, S W, 1996 The experimental earthwork on Morden Bog, Wareham, 1973 to 1990 (27th year), in M Bell et al 1996, 201–27

Hodder, I and Orton, C, 1976 *Spatial analysis in archaeology*, Cambridge

HTS: Hunting Land & Environment, 1996 Suggested methodology for preservation backfill at Anchor Terrace car park, 1–15 Southwark Bridge Road, London: report R1093/305360:HOL-01, Hunting Technical Services, Hemel Hempstead, Hertfordshire

Hunt, R, Dyer, R H and Driscoll, R, 1991 *Foundation movement and remedial underpinning in low rise buildings*, Building Research Establishment, Garston, Watford

Hunter, F and Currie, J A, 1956 Structural changes during bulk soil storage, *Journal of Soil Science* 7, 75–80

IFA: Institute of Field Archaeologists, 1994 revised 2001 *Standard and guidance for archaeological desk-based assessment*, Reading

Ingold, T, 1993 The temporality of the landscape, *World Archaeology* 25, 175–86

Institution of Civil Engineers, 1996 Planning and control of construction, in *Civil engineering procedure* (5th edition), ICE, London

Jewell, P (ed), 1963 *The experimental earthwork at Overton Down, Wiltshire, 1960*, British Association for the Advancement of Science, London

Karol, R H, 1990 *Chemical grouting*, New York

Kent, S, 1984 *Analysing activity areas: an ethnological study of the use of space*, Albuquerque, New Mexico

Koerner, R M, 1990 *Designing with geosynthetics*, 2nd edition, Englewood Cliffs, New Jersey

McGill, G, 1995 *Building on the past: a guide to the archaeology and development process*, London

Mair, R J and Wood, D M, 1987 *Pressuremeter testing: methods and interpretation*, Construction Industry Research and Information Association (CIRIA), London

Mathewson, C C, 1987 Logic-based qualitative site decay model for the preservation of archaeological sites, in *Proceedings of the interdisciplinary workshop on the physical-chemical-biological processes affecting archaeological sites* (ed C C Mathewson), US Army Engineer Waterways Experiment Station, Vicksburg, Mississippi, 227–38

Mathewson, C C and Gonzalez, T, 1988 Protection and preservation of archaeological sites through burial, in *Engineering geology of ancient works, monuments and historic sites: preservation and protection* (ed P G Marinos and G C Koukis), Rotterdam, Netherlands

Meigh, A C, 1987 *Cone penetration testing: methods and interpretation*, Construction Industry Research and Information Association (CIRIA), London

Millard, A, 1998 Bone in the burial environment, in Corfield et al 1998, 93–102

Neville, A M and Brooks, J J, 1997 *Concrete technology*, Harlow

Nielsen, R L L, 1993 *Deen City Farm Grazing, Valley Way, Mitcham, London Borough of Merton: an archaeological evaluation (site code DCF93)*, Museum of London Archaeology Service, London

Nixon, T, 1998 Practically preserved: observations on the impact of construction on urban archaeological deposits, in Corfield et al 1998, 39–46

Ove Arup: Ove Arup & Partners and the Department of Archaeology, University of York in association with B Thorpe, 1991 *York development and archaeology*, Manchester

Ove Arup: Ove Arup & Partners, 1997 The Governor's House: an engineering and archaeological strategy: internal report, Ove Arup & Partners, London

Parker-Pearson, M, 1995 Ethics and the dead in British archaeology, *The Field Archaeologist* 23

Petts, J, Rivett, M and Butler, B, 2000 *Survey of remedial techniques for land contamination in England and Wales*, R&D Technical report P401, Environment Agency R&D Dissemination Centre, c/o WRc, Franklin Road, Swindon

Pollard, A M, 1998 The chemical nature of the burial environment, in Corfield et al 1998, 60–5

Pryor, F, 1992 Current research at Flag Fen, Peterborough, *Antiquity* 66 (251), 439–57

Pugh-Smith, J and Samuels, J, 1996 *Archaeology in law*, London

Read, G F, 1997 *Sewers: rehabilitation and new construction (repair and renovation)*, London

RMC, 1985 *A practical guide to restoration*, RMC, High Street, Feltham, Middlesex TW13 4HA, London

Royal Commission, 1996 *Sustainable use of soil*, Royal Commission on Environmental Pollution 19th report, London

Schiffer, M B, 1987 *Formation processes of the archaeological record*, Albuquerque, New Mexico

Schiffer, M B and Gummerman, G J, 1977 *Conservation archaeology: a guide for cultural resource management studies*, London

Schofield, J and Malt, D (eds), 1996 *MoLAS 96: annual review for 1995*, Museum of London Archaeology Service, London

Slater, J E, 1983 *Corrosion of metals in association with concrete*, American Society for Testing Materials special technical publication 818, Philadelphia

Somerville, S H, 1988 *Control of groundwater for temporary works*, CIRIA report 113, Construction Industry Research and Information Association (CIRIA), London

Son, L H and Yuen, G C S, 1993 *Building maintenance technology*, Basingstoke

Thompson, G, 1997 The impact of engineering on buried archaeological artefacts in the UK, unpublished dissertation for the Soil Mechanics MSc, Imperial College, London

Thorne, R M, 1988 *Guidelines for the organisation of archaeological site stabilisation projects: a modelled approach*, Technical report EL-88-8, US Army Engineer Waterways Experiment Station, Vicksburg, Mississippi

Thorne, R, Fay, P M and Hester, J J, 1987 *Archaeological site preservation techniques: a preliminary review*, Technical report EL-87-3, US Army Engineer Waterways Experiment Station, Vicksburg, Mississippi

Tilly, G P, 1998 Engineering methods of minimising damage and preserving archaeological remains *in situ*, in Corfield et al 1998, 1–7

Tomlinson, M J, 1995 *Foundation design and construction* (6th edition), Harlow

US Army Corps of Engineers, 1992 *The archaeological sites protection and preservation notebook*, Environmental Impact Research Program, Waterways Experiment Station, Vicksburg, Mississippi

Wagner, D, Kropp, M, Abelskamp-Boos, K A N, Dakoronia, F, Earl, N, Ferguson, C, Fischer, W R, Hills, C C, Kars, H, Leenheer, R and Meijers, R, 1997 *Soil archive classification of European excavation sites in terms of impacts of conservability of archaeological heritage*, European Commission Contract EV5V-CT94-0516, Brussels, Belgium

Wainwright, G J, 1993 The management of change: archaeology and planning, *Antiquity* 67, 416–21

Ward, R C and Robinson, M, 1990 *Principles of hydrology*, 3rd edition, London

Water Research Council (WRC), 1990 *Water mains rehabilitation manual*, WRC, Buckinghamshire

Watson, J, 1994 *Highway construction and maintenance* (2nd edition), Harlow

Welch, J and Thomas, S, 1998 Groundwater modelling of waterlogged archaeological deposits, in Corfield et al 1998, 16–20

Weltman, A J and Little, J A, 1977 *A review of bearing pile types*, CIRIA report PG1, Construction Industry Research and Information Association (CIRIA), London

Wiltshire, P, 1997 Palynological assessment of soils and sediments, in *The over lowland investigations, Cambridgeshire, Part I: The 1996 evaluation* (ed C Evans and M Knight), 76–82, Cambridge Archaeological Unit

Winterkorn, H F and Fang, H Y (eds), 1975 *Foundation engineering handbook*, New York

Woodiwiss, S, 1998 The rural context: a view from the sticks, in Corfield et al 1998, 16–20

INDEX

Compiled by Susan Vaughan

Page numbers in **bold** denote illustrations.